Digital Activism Decoded

The New Mechanics of Change

Digital Activism Decoded

The New Mechanics of Change

Mary Joyce, editor

international debate education association

New York & Amsterdam

Published by:
International Debate Education Association
400 West 59th Street
New York, NY 10019

Library of Congress Cataloging-in-Publication Data

Digital activism decoded : the new mechanics of change / Mary Joyce,
editor.
    p. cm.
    ISBN 978-1-932716-60-3
1. Information technology--Political aspects. 2. Internet--Political
aspects. 3. Cyberspace--Political aspects. 4. Social movements. 5.
Protest movements. I. Joyce, Mary (Mary C.)
    HM851.D515 2010
    303.48'40285--dc22
                        2010012414

Design by Kathleen Hayes
Printed in the USA

 **IDEBATE Press**

Contents

Preface: The Problem with Digital Activism   vii

Introduction: How to Think About Digital Activism
   Mary Joyce   1

Part 1: Contexts: The Digital Activism Environment   15
Infrastructure: Its Transformations and Effect on Digital Activism
   Trebor Scholz   17
Applications: Picking the Right One in a Transient World
   Dan Schultz and Andreas Jungherr.   33
Devices: The Power of Mobile Phones
   Brannon Cullum   47
Economic and Social Factors: The Digital (Activism) Divide
   Katharine Brodock   71
Political Factors: Digital Activism in Closed and Open Societies
   Tom Glaisyer.   85

Part 2: Practices: Digital Actions in the Aggregate   99
Activism Transforms Digital: The Social Movement Perspective
   Anastasia Kavada.   101
Digital Transforms Activism: The Web Ecology Perspective
   Tim Hwang   119
Destructive Activism: The Double-Edged Sword of Digital Tactics
   Steven Murdoch   137

Part 3: Effects: What Is Digital Activism's Value? 149

Measuring the Success of Digital Campaigns
Dave Karpf 151

The New Casualties: Prisons and Persecution
Simon Columbus 165

Digital Politics as Usual
Rasmus Kleis Nielsen................................. 181

The Future of Advocacy in a Networked Age
Sem Devillart and Brian Waniewski...................... 197

Conclusion: Building the Future of Digital Activism
Mary Joyce.. 209

Glossary
Talia Whyte and Mary Joyce 217

About the Authors 223

Preface

The Problem with Digital Activism

Over the past few years, citizens around the world have become increasingly aware of and interested in the expanding use of digital technologies—mobile phones and Internet-enabled devices, for example—in campaigns for social and political change. These practices, which we refer to as "digital activism," have been reported by journalists, dissected by bloggers, and eagerly studied by scholars, students, activists, and enthusiasts who wish to understand and replicate the most effective tactics.

In our efforts to understand digital activism, however, we are too often presented with only anecdotes and case studies: tales of political campaigns, like Barack Obama's, that used a social network to mobilize volunteers; inspiring stories from Iran or Moldova about citizens broadcasting mobile phone videos on YouTube or giving protest updates on Twitter. Anecdotes are reported, lauded, hyped, and critiqued. Sometimes lessons and best practices are extracted that can be applied to other campaigns. The field, nonetheless, remains fragmented.

If we focus on anecdotes, we will never truly understand digital activism because the use and relevance of digital tools and tactics are constantly changing. The goal of this book is to move beyond surface anecdotes to underlying mechanics: What are the contextual factors we must consider when evaluating any case of digital activism? What conceptual framework can we use to analyze the practices of digital activism? What is the value of digital activism within our global society? While we will continue to be inspired and fascinated by cases of digital activism around the world, for understanding, we must first discover the fundamental forces that allow these actions to unfold.

Why Use the Term "Digital Activism"?

Just as the mechanics of digital activism are clouded, so is the terminology. In fact, the phrase "digital activism" is not even the consensus term for the use of digital technology in campaigning. If the term "digital activism" is contested, why do we use it in this book? Because the speed, reliability, scale, and low cost of the digital network are what enable the great scope and reach of contemporary activism. This phenomenon is what we focus on. We want a term to refer to this set of digitally networked campaigning activities—or practices—that is both exhaustive and exclusive. Exhaustive in that it encompasses *all* social and political campaigning practices that use digital network infrastructure; exclusive in that it excludes practices that are *not* examples of this type of practice.

Some terms fail to meet the criterion for exhaustiveness because they preclude relevant practices. For example, "cyber-activism," "online organizing," and "online activism" are not exhaustive because they refer only to activism on the Internet, excluding the use of mobile phones and other offline digital devices in activism—distributing digital content on thumb drives, for instance. Likewise, the phrase "social media for social change," which refers to the use of social applications like Facebook and Flickr for activism, is not exhaustive because it precludes other relevant activist applications like mobile SMS and email.

Other terms are exhaustive in that they encompass all relevant practices, but fail to be exclusive because they include irrelevant practices. "E-activism" and "e-advocacy" are earlier terms for digital campaigning practices that are derived from the word "email," in which the "e" refers to "electronic." At the advent of the Internet, the "e" preface was useful in differentiating mail sent by an electronic device, the computer, from mail sent by post, or a bound paper book from an e-book. However, the range of technologies that are electronic is far broader than those that are digital. Activists have used Dictaphones, electronic megaphones, and VHS tape recorders, but these technologies are not digital because they do not encode and transmit information as the digits 1 and 0, as is the case with a digital device. They do not make use of the low-cost scalability of the global digital network. While non-digital technologies certainly have value for activism, they will not be the subject of this book.

So far, the terminology of digital activism has referred to particular types of infrastructure, both hardware and software. Cyber-activism refers to the Internet; social media for social change refers to social software applications; e-activism refers to electronic devices. The last term that fails the exhaustive and exclusive test is different in that it refers to content, not infrastructure. "Info-activism," a term coined by the international training group Tactical Technology Collective, refers to the use of "information and communications technology to enhance advocacy work." However, as project leader Dirk Slater commented in a recent online dialogue hosted by the organization New Tactics in Human Rights: "I'd define info-activism as the strategic and deliberate use of information within a campaign. It's not necessarily digital or Internet-based, in fact it often isn't one of those two things at all."[1] While some info-activism uses digital technology, it need not. Effective info-activism could use printed flyers, stencils, or word-of-mouth. The scope of practices encompassed by info-activism is broader than those encompassed by digital activism, so the term is exhaustive but not exclusive.

In this book, we are not arguing for the preeminence of the term "digital activism" over other terms. If someone is exclusively interested in the use of the Internet for activism, he or she can and should use a term like "cyber-activism" or "online advocacy." However, we are arguing that—because it is exhaustive and exclusive—"digital activism" is the best term to discuss all instances of social and political campaigning practice that use digital network infrastructure.

Two Caveats on Bias and Certitude

Two caveats before we continue. First, a note about bias: The authors in this anthology are not dispassionate observers of digital activism. We study, analyze, and criticize digital activism because we want it to succeed. We want to see a new world in which citizens can use digital technologies to exercise their political power more effectively. We are practical idealists and we hope this book will inspire you to become one as well.

Second, though the title of this book is *Digital Activism Decoded*, it would more accurately be called "Beginning to Decode Digital Activism" or "The Extent to Which Digital Activism Has Been Decoded Thus Far." Although the current title certainly has a better ring to it, these other two more accurately reflect the position of this book in the field. Digital activism is a new practice, a new term, and a new field of study. In fact, this is the first book explicitly dedicated to the topic.

Being first is important but far from glorious. No doubt, others will improve on the work put forth in this book. No doubt, too, that some of the predictions and formulations in this book may end up being wrong or at least incomplete. Developers like to call the first version of a piece of software they release 1.0, an appellation that assumes 2.0 will follow. The field of digital activism needs foundational knowledge. We humbly present this book as the first stone and invite others to build upon and improve it.

Appreciation

We are unable to acknowledge all those who have made the publication of this book possible, but we would like to thank a few. We would like to thank our editor, Eleanora von Dehsen, for her kindness, wisdom, and energy in shepherding this book from concept to publication, and Martin Greenwald at the Open Society Institute/iDebate Press for believing in this project.

For reading early chapter drafts and providing invaluable advice and insight, we would like to thank Nishant Shah of the Centre for Internet and Society in Bangalore, Amy Sample Ward of NetSquared, Louise Swan and Ellen Liu of the Open Society Institute's Health Media Initiative, Esra'a Al Shafei of Mideast Youth, Michael Anti, Hapee de Groot of Hivos, Dirk Slater of Tactical Technology Collective, Rick Bahague of Computer Professionals' Union, Helmi Noman, Georg Neumann of Transparency International, Kristin Antin of New Tactics in Human Rights, Alaa Abd El Fattah, Katrin Verclas of MobileActive.org, and Dan McQuillan of internet.artizans.

Finally, we would like to thank our families and friends for their support and patience through the long hours we spent staring at our computer screens instead of paying attention to them while writing this book. We hope it was worth the effort.

Mary Joyce
New Orleans
February 12, 2010

Notes

1. http://www.newtactics.org/node/6179 (accessed January 20, 2010).

Introduction: How to Think About Digital Activism

Mary Joyce

The goal of this introduction is to provide a framework for thinking about digital activism. We begin by identifying the infrastructure, economic, social, and political factors that define the environment in which digital activists operate. Next, we discuss activism practices themselves, both how they are currently understood in the narrative form of case study and how they might be codified in the future as foundational knowledge. Finally, we lay out the range of opinions on the value of digital activism and explain why determining value conclusively is still difficult. In this Introduction, we will discuss both what is known and what is unknown about digital activism—the mechanics of which are just beginning to be understood.

Context: The Digital Activism Environment

Wouldn't it be nice if understanding digital activism were as easy as riding a bike? For most people, digital activism is a foreign concept, while bike riding is clear, concrete, and defined by personal experience. The two are not so different, however. Just as the infrastructure of bike riding is based on the network of paths, highways, and trails over which the bike is pedaled, the infrastructure of digital activism is based on the digital network. Both bike riding and digital activism are "practices"—habitual activities that occur within a particular context and have certain effects. Like bike riding, we determine the value of digital activism based on aggregate effect, which is not always easy to determine.

The context of digital activism refers both to the digital technology that is used in a given activism campaign and to the economic, social, and political context in which such technology use occurs. Digital technology infrastructure—the combination of networks, code, applications, and devices that make up the physical infrastructure of digital activism—is a starting point but not an ending point. Differences in economic, social, and political factors ultimately alter how activists use this technology.

TECHNOLOGICAL INFRASTRUCTURE

The infrastructure of digital activism is based on the digital network—an interconnected group of devices that use digital code to transmit information. The beauty of networks is that connectivity is distributed. Networks do not connect us only to the center, they link us to each other as well. And, when large numbers of citizens are able to more easily connect to one another, to send and receive original content, and to coordinate action, they are able to create effective political movements.

Networks can be fashioned of different physical materials—physical materials matter. The difference in materials from country to country provides a great example of how the interplay of infrastructure, economic, social, and political factors leads to different digital activism outcomes. Modern cable infrastructure, such as fiber optic, which transmits a signal more quickly, is more expensive than older and slower cable—which might be made of copper. Thus, those living in rich countries are likely to have faster Internet connections than those living in poorer countries. Politics plays a role, too: in many developing countries, particularly in Africa, state-owned firms have historically monopolized Internet service, leading to higher prices. As a result, people in richer countries are usually more able to participate in digital activism because of the cost and quality of Internet connections available to them.

If the differentiator of digital networks is material, the unifier is code—the series of the digits 1 and 0 that transmit all information on the Internet. Digital code is the universal medium of digital activism. If an activist in Gaza wants to upload a mobile phone video so it can be watched by a college student in Minneapolis, digital code transmits those sounds and images. If an activist in the Philippines starts a Facebook group opposing the corruption of a local official, Filipino expatriates from Abu Dhabi to London can join the group and coordinate in English or their native Tagalog. In a 2009 article in *The New Republic*, technology theorist Lawrence Lessig of Harvard University described the nature of digital as "perfect copies, freely made." If you create any piece of content and upload it to a digital network, a copy of that content will become immediately transmissible to anyone else in the world with Internet access. The whole world speaking one language—that is the power of digital code.

Even though we use digital networks to send each other 1s and 0s, we don't think of digital activism in terms of code. We think of it in terms of applications, the software programs that interpret those 1s and 0s into meaningful information. Fortunately, digital infrastructure is, according to Harvard law professor Jonathan Zittrain, "generative." People can easily develop applications that operate on top of the network and create content using those applications, both of which may not have been intended by their creators. The inventers of Facebook, a group of American college students, probably did not see it as a tool for activists around the world, but it is nevertheless used for that purpose. Likewise, the Silicon Valley technologists who founded Twitter did not imagine that their service would be used to broadcast protests in Moldova. While dedicated activist applications and open source software also play a role, most digital activists co-opt commercial applications like Facebook, Twitter, Blogger, and YouTube to do their work. It is through these applications that most of us define our use of network infrastructure.

Applications are the most visible element of digital activism and many handbooks, blogs, and training sessions focus on the use of specific applications (also called "apps") for campaigns for political and social change. However, applications are a poor foundation for the study of digital activism: They change constantly, are popular because of media hype as much as actual utility, and have outcomes intensely affected by other contextual factors that differ greatly from campaign to campaign. Applications are only a part of the digital activism environment. We are most aware of them because they define our experience of digital activism, not because they are more important than other factors.

We access applications on "end devices," the piece of hardware that connects the user to the network. In the world of digital activism, the most common end devices are currently the computer and mobile phone. Computers currently allow for a wider variety of activism applications than mobile phones because they allow users to connect to all the applications on the Internet while most mobile phones are limited to SMS and calling. Yet, as the release of Apple's iPad tablet and the rise of Internet-enabled smart phones illustrates, the differences between these types of devices is becoming more blurred as computers become more like mobile phones and mobile phones gain the capacity of computers. This change results in more powerful and cheaper devices for activists and thus a greater capacity to use digital infrastructure for their goals of political and social change.

CONTEXTUAL FACTORS

Digital technology is the infrastructure of the digital activism environment. Economic, social, and political factors determine whether and how people use this infrastructure. The economic power of digital activists—their ability to buy digital goods and services—affects their digital activism practices. For example, because more individuals in wealthy countries are able to pay for Internet services, these markets are more profitable for firms to enter, leading to greater competition and lower prices. As a result, more people can become involved in activism. Economics also affects the type of hardware activists use. Computers are expensive; consequently, these high-functionality devices are more accessible to those with financial resources. Such access also affects digital activism participation rates. This does not preclude people of limited financial resources from taking part in digital activism. Because of the recent dramatic expansion of worldwide mobile phone use, these tools (which admittedly have a more limited range of functions) have been employed for effective digital activism in many parts of the world. Through cyber cafés, individuals who do not own a computer can use one for an hourly fee. But cost and inconvenience may limit their activities.

When thinking about the effect of economic factors on digital activism, we must consider the individual within the context of a larger system: What digital tools can the individual activist afford and what digital tools are available in the geographic market that she has access to? How does the economic situation of her physical location affect her activism choices?

Societal norms can also greatly influence whether and how a person uses digital technology for activism. Just as there are expectations about what clothing one should wear or what one should do with leisure time, there are expectations about the practices associated with digital activism. These expectations often differ according to the social group to which an individual belongs and are based on characteristics such as age, gender, religion, education, ethnicity, or socioeconomic status. Katharine Brodock's essay on the digital activism divide contains a story from Uganda where girls at one school rarely use the public computers because access is given on a first come first service basis. The boys always rush to grab a machine while the girls, who are expected to be ladylike, walk to the lab and do not get a seat. In considering the social factors that affect involvement in digital activism, we need to look at both the digital perspective, and that of activism. Expectations are involved not only in who should use technology but also in who should take part in political campaigning.

Political factors also influence activism. In democratic and semi-democratic societies, where citizens have meaningful influence over the actions of their government, the political context of digital activism can be understood in terms of law and regulation. However, repressive and authoritarian governments do not limit themselves to legal channels when shaping the digital activism environment. In these countries, even activists who have access to digital technologies have difficulties using them because of government-imposed limitations. These governments track online political speech and block applications used by digital activists. Often such online obstruction leads to offline persecution and even imprisonment.

We must remember that, while in some cases governments affect activists directly, as in the case of persecution of individuals, most often the influence of government is felt through other government structures and actions. Government investment and regulation determine the quality, and sometimes the price, of access to digital infrastructure. Laws protecting civil rights (or failing to do so) create a legal backbone for social norms around activism practice. Although all four elements of the digital activism environment—infrastructure, economic, social, and political—influence one another, this is particularly true of the political. Government is the ultimate source of authority in most societies and its influence on activism is similarly widespread.

Because context is important to understanding digital activism, we begin with five essays on the topic. The first three address technological infrastructure. Trebor Scholz's essay, "Infrastructure: Its Transformations and Effect on Digital Activism," takes a historical perspective. It describes the evolution of digital activism infrastructure from the creation of ARPANET in 1969 to the rise of the commercial Web in the mid-1990s and social media applications in the 2000s.

"Applications: Picking the Right One in a Transient World," by Dan Schultz and Andreas Jungherr, delves further into the value of applications. Speaking from the perspective of digital activism practitioners, it offers advice on choosing the best application given the transient nature of tools used in cyberspace. In "Devices: The Power of Mobile Phones," Brannon Cullum looks at end devices and, because most of the book focuses on computer-based Internet applications, is devoted solely to the use of mobile phones in activism.

The last two articles in this section discuss elements of the digital activism environment beyond infrastructure. "Economic and Social Factors: The Digital (Activism) Divide," by Katharine Brodock, addresses how inequality of access and skills, as well as the intentional obstruction of government censorship, limits participation in digital activism. "Political Factors: Digital Activism in Closed and Open Societies," by Tom Glaisyer, delves more deeply into the political factors first addressed in Brodock's chapter. Glaisyer's essay describes how digital activism outcomes depend greatly on whether a country is free and politically open or repressive and politically closed.

Practices: Digital Actions in the Aggregate

What do we think of when we hear the term "digital activism practices"? We think of activism campaigns with a goal of social or political change that use digital technology. We think of recent news stories about digital activism: the grainy cell phone videos of the Iranian protests uploaded to YouTube, or a photo of the protesters in Chişinău, Moldova, also demonstrating against an allegedly corrupt election and called together by social applications like Twitter, SMS, and the blogging platform LiveJournal. Maybe we think of a personal experience, like joining Barack Obama's social network, MyBO, during the 2008 campaign.

Looking at digital activism practice through the lens of specific case studies and anecdotes has value, as activists can identify tactics that worked in a particular case and replicate those tactics if their own context is similar. Case studies are, in essence, stories; we, as human beings, find stories both entertaining and easy to understand. They are often dramatic and emotionally charged: thousands of people in the streets, a clash between freedom and oppression, people power on the rise.

Case studies also form the current foundation for the study of digital activism. Most of the first books and articles were based on detailed analyses of particular cases of digital activism. The anthology *Cyberactivism: Online Activism in Theory and Practice* (2003) contained case studies about World Bank protesters, feminist activists, and Mexico's indigenous Zapatista movement. In his Foreword to *Cyberprotest: New Media, Citizens and Social Movements"* (2004), Peter Daulgren of Sweden's Lund University, noted specifically that case study allowed the field to move beyond mere conjecture:

> Building largely on a series of case studies . . . this collection moves beyond generalizations and speculation by addressing concretely the implications that ICTs [information and communication technologies] have for various forms of contemporary social movements.

Scholars have questioned the reliance on case studies, yet they are still central to our understanding of digital activism practice because the field is beset with a two-part data problem. First, there simply is not enough data available to scholars, both because data have not been collected and because digital activism is a relatively new practice and its instances are still limited. Second, data that do exist (such as usage patterns from social media platforms) have not yet been rigorously analyzed. The field needs to create foundational knowledge by using rigorous quantitative analysis to test theories based on case studies and qualitative information. The first step in creating such knowledge is to analyze digital actions in the aggregate, rather than focus on an endless number of individual cases.

Scholars use two types of strategies to create this foundational knowledge. The first considers the activism elements of digital activism to be primary and takes theories that describe offline activism and applies them to digital practice. Writers in this school see digital technology as altering existing activism practices. In the first essay of the second section, "Activism Transforms Digital: The Social Movement Perspective," Anastasia Kavada describes social movement theory and explains how digital technology is creating new practices and possibilities for these movements.

The second strategy considers the digital element as primary and takes theories that explain the digital environment and applies them to activism practices. Writers in this school believe the unique qualities of the digital environment are transforming a variety of social practices, of which activism is just one example. Tim Hwang takes this approach in "Digital Transforms Activism: The Web Ecology Perspective." He introduces the new research area of Web ecology, which seeks to study online social forces that form the foundation of both cultural fads and political activism.

Opinions vary greatly about what a valid activist cause is and what constitutes positive political and social change. Although the general tenor of this book is optimistic about the potential of digital activism, certainly viewing digital practice with a skeptical eye is warranted, as is openness about its shortcomings. The last essay of this section addresses the "dark side" of digital activism. In "Destructive Activism: The Double-Edged Sword of Digital Tactics," Steven Murdoch lays out a taxonomy of digital activism tactics that are destructive and disruptive and asks important questions about how we determine whether a tactic is justified.

Effects: What Is Digital Activism's Value?

The value of digital activism is not always clear, even when an evaluation is based on the objective effects of digital practices. Taken in isolation, the three chapters of the previous section imply very different values of digital activism practice. Anastasia Kavada's article discusses how digital technology is strengthening social movements by giving them new tools and capacities. Tim Hwang's essay sketches a new world in which new tools not only assist but transform the way activists can interact with one another and with supporters. Yet Steven Murdoch's article illuminates a world of malicious and sometimes illegal behavior in which digital technology allows for new forms of harassment and obstruction. These chapters raise important questions about the ultimate value of digital activism.

Just as over-reliance on case studies and anecdotes plagues the study of digital activism practices, it also muddles the determination of the value of these practices. Whatever value one wishes to assign to digital practice, an anecdote is available and—unfortunately—there is likely also an anecdote to support the opposing point of view. Rather than start a debate by arguing that digital activism does or will have a particular value, we will first sketch the range of opinions on the topic and then present a variety of arguments in each field.

We can identify three basic perspectives on the value of digital activism: optimists, pessimists, and persistents. All three categories should be understood as broad and complex. The goal of this framework is to map the range of opinion on the value of digital activism in a way that makes the topic more accessible, not to pigeonhole individuals who take part in this debate.

With this in mind, the first two categories imply a basic positive or negative outlook on the potential of digital technology to change the distribution of political power. While optimists believe that digital activism will alter existing political hierarchies and empower citizens, pessimists believe that these technologies are just as likely to be used to exert illegitimate authority or encourage chaos. Like optimists, pessimists also believe that digital technology will have a significant impact on the world, but they see the technology as morally neutral, equally useful for constructive and destructive purposes. Pessimists use the moral neutrality argument to underline the possibility of destructive behavior and to counter the optimists, who tend to be more optimistic about human nature in general and see the moral nature of the Internet as a reflection of the moral nature of its users. Optimists note that most people on the Internet seek entertainment, communication, information, or commerce, not destruction.

The third category—"persistent"—refers to those who see neither salvation nor damnation in digital technology, but instead believe that little will change and previous political power distributions will "persist." Persistents may be optimistic or pessimistic about digital technology, but they don't believe it matters very much for activism. In this way, they differ from the other two categories as their optimism or pessimism about digital activism's outcomes is less important in defining their intellectual identity than is their opinion about what author David Weinberger calls "web exceptionalism." Simply put, they do not believe that the Web—and by extension digital activism—is exceptional. The same rules of politics still apply and technology will not change existing power structures, either for good or for ill.

The optimistic view, as put forth by such scholars as Yochai Benkler, Mark Pesce, Clay Shirky, and Graeme Kirkpatrick, is founded on two basic principles. First, according to Benkler, Pesce, and Shirky, the networked nature of the digital world allows for people to communicate and take action outside of—and sometimes in opposition to—traditional hierarchical power structures. In a hierarchy, those at the top have power over those at the bottom; networks have a much flatter power distribution, with authority defined by peer-to-peer relationships. The hope is that the nature of power in the digital network will change the nature of power in the real world as digital networks become ever more integrated into our lives.

The second principle of digital optimism, as put forth elegantly by Graeme Kirkpatrick in his book, *Technology and Social Power* (2008), is that technology is "socially constructed." This means that users construct the value and meaning of technology by how they use it, for example, co-opting an entertainment platform like YouTube and using it to transmit alternative political content. In this way, the optimistic view proposes a more just and egalitarian future, along with a means of achieving this future that empowers the ordinary user to create meaning.

Many of the pessimistic views of technology, on the other hand, hinge on the fear of anti-democratic control of technology. The journalist and blogger Evgeny Morozov is one of the most well-known proponents of this view. He points out that digital technology provides new methods of control, surveillance, and persecution for repressive governments, as well as the ability to empower destructive individuals like hackers and terrorists to co-ordinate their actions and use the network to attack targets that would previously have been beyond their reach.

This argument is substantial. The physical infrastructure of the Internet exists within territorial boundaries, even if its capacities are virtual. It is at the level of physical infrastructure that governments can block access to content and track the online actions of citizens. Networks also enhance the effectiveness of surveillance as all content can now be directed through the same gateways and "read" as it passes by, a convenience unavailable in the days of paper notes and whispered messages. Following this logic, digital technology may endanger activists more than it helps them.

Similar to the pessimists, the persistents are not too impressed by digital activism. They believe that networked technology signals a change in the degree—though not the inherent nature—of activism practice. It simply makes existing offline tactics like mobilization, organization, and message dissemination more effective. Persistents like Marshall Ganz, an architect of President Obama's grassroots organizing campaign in 2008, focus on the fact that digital tools facilitate activities that were already possible offline, only more slowly or at greater cost. For every e-petition, a paper petition could also have been circulated. For every Facebook group, a house party could have been held. We can all acknowledge that, because institutions of political and social power exist offline, all digital campaigns must at some point make the leap into the real world if they are to be successful. Persistents take this logic one step further. They do not believe that the cumulative digital effect of bigger, cheaper, faster, and further will lead to fundamentally different kinds of activism, only to potentially improved versions of current ones.

Before we determine the value of the effects of digital practices, we must decide how to measure those effects. The first essay of the third section, Effects: What Is Digital Activism's Value?, Dave Karpf's "Measuring the Success of Digital Campaigns," describes the difficulty of measuring the results of digital activism campaigns. While optimistic about the possibilities of digital activism, he stresses the importance of the time-honored methods of the persistents and encourages activists to begin with classic organizing strategy: Let the goal of the campaign determine how you will measure the campaign's effectiveness.

None of the essays in this book argue in favor of the most radical pessimist vision, that digital technology will hurt activists more than it helps them by empowering the forces of oppression and exploitation. However, the next article in this section is exclusively devoted to digital activism's unintended negative consequences. Drawing on new research on imprisoned bloggers around the world, "The New Casualties: Prisons and Persecution," by Simon Columbus, addresses the harm that repressive regimes can do to digital activists who dare to oppose them. Sometimes, this persecution is carried out through effective use of digital technology.

"Digital Politics as Usual," by Rasmus Kleis Nielsen, more fully embodies the viewpoint of the persistents. The basic argument of his chapter is that we need to give up the idea that digital technologies will bring about a radical break with the past. Nielsen critiques the "great potential" discourse of the optimists, who claim that the changes digital activism will bring are forever just around the corner, and instead encourages a thorough review of current digital activism practice. Based on his own research of American political campaigns, Nielsen suggests that digital technology has not radically changed politics but is, rather, a "practical prosthetic" on previous organizing practices.

Finally, in "The Future of Advocacy in a Networked Age," futurists Sem Devillart and Brian Waniewski take a much more optimistic view. In a speculative essay they outline the difficulties currently faced by advocacy groups and activists and then examine how networks can help overcome these difficulties and bring into being new forms of activism that are more in tune with the digital age. They sketch an idealistic future for digital activism, one in which the Internet increases mutual understanding between advocates and their opponents.

This book attempts to aggregate current knowledge on digital activism, but many gaps remain, data are still lacking, and systemic analysis is scarce. The effectiveness of digital activism practice is most likely to improve if foundational knowledge is generated and that knowledge is transmitted to activists through a network that engages all stakeholders. Anecdote must be replaced by exhaustive data aggregation and rigorous analyses that explain the parameters of digital practice beyond the latest hyped application or networked "revolution." This knowledge must then be transmitted to practitioners so that theory may be put into practice. Digital technology does not determine our political future, we do. To paraphrase the Chinese activist Xiao Qiang, because the fate of digital activism is uncertain, we the idealists must act.

PART 1

Contexts: The Digital Activism Environment

```
01111001
01101111
01110101
01110010
01110111
01101111
01110010
01101100
01100100
01110100
01101111
01100011
01101000
01100001
01101110
01100111
01100101
```

Infrastructure: Its Transformations and Effect on Digital Activism

Trebor Scholz

The Internet has evolved into a single global matrix where activists gain real-time international attention for their struggles. More than forty years ago, the Net started out as a military-scientific project, consisting of no more than four university nodes. When officially opened for commercial use in the mid-1990s, however, the Net had grown to be a large international network. Many activists initially rejected this commercialization; today such dismissal of the profit-driven services online would simply disadvantage political activists. The history of the Internet is full of cultural experiments, with declarations of independence from corporatist forces and stories about empowerment. Such empowerment devolved not only to activists and libertarians but also to dictators and others of their ilk.

1969–1994: A Closed Research Network

Many changes have occurred since the first nodes of ARPANET, the predecessor of the Internet, were linked together in 1969. At that time, computers were enormous, clunky, and prohibitively expensive—one purpose of ARPANET, which was one of the projects of the Department of Defense's Advanced Research Projects Agency, was to allow more scientists to work with these scarce machines. Instead of putting the networked computers to work on complex calculations, researchers turned ARPANET against the intentions of its creators by using it to communicate with one another. This was the single biggest unintended consequence of ARPANET.

ARPANET's "network mail," a precursor to today's email, was not exclusively used to discuss research—it also helped distribute messages against the Vietnam War, hosted discussions about the Watergate scandal, and ultimately the resignation of Pres. Richard Nixon.

At the same time, however, ARPANET also became a tool that helped the Pentagon shadow political activists. The American public became aware of ARPANET in the early 1970s—two years after it was activated. National media alerted them to the role of this research network in government surveillance. During the political unrest of the late 1960s, military intelligence had started to collect information about the location of firehouses and police precincts in dozens of American cities. One Pentagon official decided to add local troublemakers to this map. After the story broke in 1972, the Pentagon was ordered by a judge to destroy all related files. As was later revealed, however, the Pentagon used ARPANET to move these files to a new location in direct violation of the court order.

Since its inception, the Internet has helped to both control and empower citizens. At the outset, ARPANET provided a communication forum for male, Caucasian, middle-class scientists with a Department of Defense contract. The ARPANET was not the only networking solution available at the time, however. Several alternative and more open communication systems were on hand. Usenet, for example, was nicknamed "the people's ARPANET," because it offered easy access to networked communication for anyone with a dial-up connection.

In 1991, ARPANET became more available to the public when it was taken over by the National Science Foundation. Military restrictions no longer applied, thus allowing ARPANET to expand beyond the defense community. Foreign networks could also join, with Japan among the first. In 1987, the first Chinese connection was established and tested by sending an email from the Technical University in Beijing to the University Karlsruhe in Germany. Throughout Europe, the number of Internet sites skyrocketed in the early 1990s.

But military declassification was not enough. For broader reach, the network also needed a commonly agreed upon language, a set of protocols that computers worldwide could use to communicate with one another. Accordingly, many governments and countless organizations, globally, had to agree to use one specific language, one protocol suite. TCP/IP became the agreed-upon language that defined how information on the Internet transferred from computer to computer across national borders.

From the early 1990s on, people in their living rooms, basements, libraries, and schools not only started to use the Internet in large numbers, they also co-shaped it. Roughly two decades were needed for the circle of network users to achieve substantial international reach.

In his book *From Counterculture to Cyberculture*, Fred Turner notes that United States right-wing powerbrokers like Newt Gingrich also embraced the Internet in the early 1990s; Gingrich and others saw that it increased the power of economic elites, helped build new businesses, and enabled the reevaluation of traditional forms of governance.[1] A few years later, Tim Berners-Lee, the co-inventor of the World Wide Web, the system of interlinked hypertext documents that is part of the Internet, called on all users to be ethically and morally aware of what they are doing because they are the ones who are creating the Web.[2]

1995-2000: Commercial Takeover and Standardization of the Internet

On May Day 1995, the National Science Foundation decommissioned the hardware backbone of the Internet and officially handed it over to commercial uses. At that point, Dutch media critic Geert Lovink claimed that California-style cyber-commercialization signaled the closing of the American Internet; the doors were shut and the keys handed over to the kings of infotainment: Disney, AOL, CNN, and the phone company MCI.[3]

While there were significant changes, the Internet did not go to mercantile hell in the late 1990s; but the experiments with digital activism and the creation of independent, noncommercial enclaves received less media attention. In those early days of the Web, design was anything but generic: Web pages were pumped up with blinking visual elements, they were often self-made, hand-coded, and sometimes had huge font sizes, odd colors, or scrolling visual elements because of human error. Web design was frequently playful as well as experimental and very few pages looked alike. Such design was the exact opposite of Tim Berners-Lee's first Web page, which was very precise and orderly.

By the mid-1990s, innovation had shifted from the development of standards and protocols toward business plans and marketing skills. The American writer Nick Carr noted:

> By the end of 1995, half of all sites bore .com addresses, and by mid-1996 commercial sites represented nearly 70 percent of the total. Three decades after the [cultural and political rebellion of the] Summer of Love [in 1967] young people began flocking to San Francisco once again, but they didn't come to listen to free verse or drop acid. They came to make a killing [financially speaking].[4]

Tim Berners-Lee cautioned that the Web is not just about buying books from Amazon.com and added that it is also not some "idealized space where we must remove our shoes, eat only fallen fruit, and eschew commercialization."[5] Business did not turn the Internet into a dead end for activists, but geeks, hackers, squatters, and tinkerers got much less attention and fewer headlines. The dotcom hype was the official news. Playful creativity and cultural experimentation, substantive content, Internet art, and experimentation with identity did not fade away, but they were much less in the limelight.

This move toward commercialism was not just a shift from the search for protocols to the establishment of speculative business plans, it was also a shift from individually designed websites, which were hosted by small Internet service providers, to large, centrally hosted, corporate service platforms. In 1994, "free" Web hosting services, including GeoCities, traded space on their servers for the placement of banner ads on a user's Web page. Countless personal home pages emerged and unwieldy do-it-yourself Web design was slowly taken over by customizable templates provided by LiveJournal or Blogger. The plethora of Web services available during the Internet boom of the early and mid-1990s narrowed substantially during the dotcom crash of 2000, which left only a few e-businesses standing. By the early twenty-first century, the great majority of customers were using the services offered by very few enterprises. Attention, which had initially been distributed over thousands of websites, slowly started to focus on a handful of convenient, standardized sites. Today, half of all Web traffic is concentrated on only 10 websites.

At first, access to information appeared far more profitable than online interaction. Tim Berners-Lee recalls that throughout the early 1990s the developers of Web browsers designed features that allowed access to information rather than facilitation of collaboration. "Putting as much effort into the collaborative side of the Web didn't seem to promise that million-fold multiplier," wrote Berners-Lee.[6] Amazon.com, which launched in 1994 as an online bookseller, did not offer collaborative features but did allow customers to self-publish book reviews on its website. The first Weblogs, created around 1994, also allowed for self-publishing online. They were part link collections, part public diaries, but even comment sections were a second thought.

Despite many warnings similar to the ones voiced by Carr, Lovink, and Berners-Lee, corporate interests had fully colonized the Internet by the mid-1990s. Not unlike the model of media ownership in the nineteenth and twentieth centuries, today the online environments with the highest traffic are owned by a handful of corporations. If you want your video to get seen by large numbers of people, it has to be on YouTube. If you would like your micro-blog post to be read, you have to post it on Twitter. While activists can make use of countless noncommercial online services like Identi.ca, they reach the largest audience only on those money-driven social blockbusters.

In the 1990s, artists and activists took on projects that experimented with issues of commerce and autonomy. For many activists of the early 1990s, the Net represented a utopian place where an alternative and perhaps even autonomous world could thrive. In Amsterdam, in early 1994 the artist Marleen Sticker cofounded Digitale Stad (DGS), envisioned as an "electronic town hall" that used the metaphor of the city to structure its online presence. The project was supported by grants from the city. Hosting as much information as possible, this social experiment was meant to represent the city of Amsterdam and make information from local government accessible to citizens—who could learn about local politicians and discuss policies. According to social media expert Reinde Rustema, newsgroups debated urban planning, crime, drugs, and art in Amsterdam. Digitale Stad did not, however, simply give power to institutions that already had a great deal of influence offline. Instead, the project aimed to equally represent resource-poor organizations—in particular, those supporting artists, immigrants, refugees, and children.[7] For those without Net access, the founders set up computer terminals in museums, libraries, and cafés throughout the Dutch capital. DGS, in its original form, came to a halt when the funding ran out.

Some of these noncommercial Internet experiments continued for a long time. In November 1999, activists got together to block Seattle streets and make their disapproval of the World Trade Organization (WTO) public. They stunned the WTO with carnival-like street performances and technological fireworks. They asserted that the WTO was merely an instrument of multinational corporations that harm small, economically developing countries. The interests of the owners of mainstream newspapers and TV stations, however, were at odds with the activists, who had experienced media distortion of their message through systematic neglect and bias many times. Commercial journalists had, for example, repeatedly underreported the number of people attending demonstrations. Activists knew that the mainstream media would scarcely report their protests and what coverage they did receive would likely misrepresent the reasons for their protest. Consequently, they founded the Independent Media Center, also referred to as Indymedia, as their own Internet-based broadcast channel. Professor Dorothy Kidd refers to the work of Indymedia as an "end-run around the information gatekeepers" with the goal of producing autonomous media.[8] To this day, Indymedia's websites allow anyone to publicize their news stories (from text and photo to video). Everybody can challenge the claims by the mainstream media, make their own voice heard, and become a citizen journalist. Citizen journalism sites like Indymedia or the South Korean OhMyNews do not make the mass media obsolete, but they do challenge their ability to shape public opinion.

Since the late 1990s, activists and governments have started to use the Net to form international perception of military conflicts. In 1999, Indymedia reported that NATO attacked Serbia to stop the imminent genocide of Kosovar Albanians by Pres. Slobodan Milosevic's troops. NATO described its bombing offensive as a "humanitarian intervention," while others referred to it as the "first Internet war." Milosevic cracked down on all dissenting voices, including the independent radio station B92, which he tried to force off the air. In May 2000, Serbian government troops seized all of B92's radio equipment, but they overlooked its Internet broadcasting capabilities. B92's programming continued online.

The Kosovo War was accompanied by reports of mayhem and destruction on mailing lists such as <nettime> where one Serb, writing under the pseudonym "insomnia," posted highly emotional accounts of what he (or she) saw right at that moment out of the window. Kosovar Albanians were barely heard from because they did not have Net access. For those with network access, such lists and Internet radio allowed for real-time, transnational attention. Today, <nettime> and Indymedia are still in operation but social networking services like Facebook receive considerably more attention.

2001-Present: Social Media, Customization, and the Participatory Turn

Contrary to common myths, Web 2.0 was not the first platform used by individuals to tell their stories. From its very beginnings, the Internet gave people a public voice. The ease and scale of participation, however, have expanded drastically in the last 40 years and especially during the past 15 years. The dotcom boom (and ultimate crash) of the mid-to-late 1990s was positive in many ways; it channeled substantial resources to dotcom companies, which developed technologies that would eventually significantly reduce the number of steps required from opening your browser to posting text, photos, or even videos.

Going online became easier and the term "social Web" came into vogue. Three historical milestones mark the history of the Web. First, the sudden and surprising adaptation of "network mail" on ARPANET in the 1970s; second, the astonishing success of the Mosaic Web browser as a "window into cyberspace" in the mid-1990s, which secured the success of the World Wide Web; third, the remarkable popularity of technologies and phenomena recently associated with social media. A fourth significant milestone has been the growth in the use mobile telephones to access the Web. More people now own mobile phones in economically developing countries than in the United States and Europe combined. Many of these phones have Internet capability—the digital divide is not what it used to be.

The increased participatory potential of the commercial services developed in the early 2000s proved extremely useful to activists. In 2002, Scott Heiferman launched a website that allowed individuals to go online to arrange meetings with others offline. This site, Meetup.com, was inspired by political scientist Robert D. Putnam's bestseller *Bowling Alone*. The book looks at the decline of social capital in post–World War II United States. Putnam claimed that civic participation, churchgoing, union membership, altruism, and voting declined precipitously in the United States during the decades following the war. With Meetup.com, Heiferman aimed to revitalize local communities and counteract the social malaise documented by Putnam. Meetup.com was vital to Howard Dean's campaign for the Democratic presidential nomination in 2004. Meetup.com gathered some hundred forty thousand supporters on the site; the Dean campaign also used it to organize volunteers who'd go door-to-door, write personal letters to likely voters, host meetings, and distribute flyers. Meetup.com is a good example for the growing trend toward activism on social networking platforms.

In 2003, several anonymous bloggers started to report from inside embattled Iraq. Under the name Riverbend, a young woman wrote about the political changes and the impact of the war on her family. On his blog "Where is Raed?"(later published as a book, *The Clandestine Diary of an Ordinary Iraqi*), a 29-year-old architect began writing under the pseudonym Salam Pax.[9] These blogs were written in English, which greatly widened their global reach and opened a window on the Iraqi perspective on the U.S. invasion of their country. Salam Pax captured the readers of his blog with droll language, passages about the music of Massive Attack and Bjork, descriptions of the lead-up to the war, the invasion, and the months immediately following. On March 27, 2003, he wrote: "[The bombardment] has become the soundtrack of our lives. You wake up to the sound of bombardment; you brush your teeth to the rhythm of the anti-aircraft rat-tattats. Then there is the attack, which is timed exactly with your lunchtime." He kept on blogging, enraging and electrifying many in the West who read and commented on his site. Using the blogware Blogger (now owned by Google), Salam Pax was able to write anonymously and receive hundreds of comments.

The destabilizing voices of bloggers in countries with repressive regimes like Malaysia or the United Arab Emirates created alternative streams of information and levels of participation in media that were previously impossible. Hitherto, such governments controlled the mass media, which allowed them to limit what their citizens knew and believed, but Weblogs can challenge entrenched governments.

China is good example of the political effects of new social media. The Chinese Ministry for the Information Industry "protects" network providers with international Internet connections by blocking websites that it labels as "trash." Because of the decentralized architecture of the Internet, however, such attempts to censor the Internet do not completely work. Perfect control over what citizens access online is impossible. In 2005, two art students from Guangzhou used a Webcam to record themselves lip-synching the Back Street Boys in their dorm room. They uploaded the video to YouTube, where it was viewed by millions of people. While these clips do not contain a hidden activist message, their video did break through the control mechanisms of the Chinese government.

In the first years of the twenty-first century, social networking services like MySpace (2003), Hi5 (2003), and Facebook (2005) became popular. The Facebook group "Support the Monk's Protest in Burma" (begun by an American tourist who was in Burma at the time of one protest) illustrates the value of such outlets for activists. Since 1962, Burma has lived under military rule—each time citizens protested or rioted, the ruling junta closed the borders and asked all journalists to leave before mercilessly cracking down on the protesters, killing hundreds. In 2007, antigovernment protests erupted once again but this time it was significantly harder to prevent acts of witness bearing because a small group of Burmese sent photos and videos from inside Burma to the British Broadcasting Corporation (BBC) via File Transfer Protocol, a standard network protocol used to exchange files over the Internet. Thousands of people became aware of the protests in part through this user-submitted material. They joined the "Support the Monk's Protest in Burma" Facebook group, which helped to widely distribute documentary images, videos, and photos all across the Web. These small acts of digital activism did not end the rule of the military, but they did direct worldwide attention to the repressive regime in Burma and may have forestalled an even more violent reaction to the dissenters. On the other hand, the Burmese government was able to simply shut down all communication, including cell phone communication, just days into the conflict.

The debate over the value of new social media infrastructure for activism is not limited to questions of the value of commercial tools or services. Some argue that digital activism is merely "click activism," or "slacktivism," a kind of liberal catharsis during lunch break that gives participants the impression that they have done something about the issues when, in fact, their online action had no offline effect at all. Very few who join political Facebook groups become involved in long-term political campaigns. In fairness, no Facebook group can be expected to ameliorate or resolve world political situations—be they Burmese government violence or some other humanitarian crisis. Are such online forums effective at all? It makes sense to temper expectations of such Facebook groups, but, at the same time, we should not lightly dismiss such nano-activism. The best course would be to carefully assess the value of each individual case of digital activism.

In some cases, the mere popularity of a platform makes it valuable to activists. Ethan Zuckerman, fellow at the Berkman Center for Internet and Society, writes that because services like YouTube have a wide user base, governments find it politically difficult to block them without unintentionally upsetting large groups of their citizens. In his blog essay, "Internet Censorship: How Cute Cats Can Help," he argues that shutting down YouTube, for example, is a highly visible act. Individuals who may not even think of themselves as activists, insert their messages into a stream of entertainment, such as photos of cute cats, on Facebook or the discussion board site 4Chan. Their messages are far less likely to be edited or revised there, where censorship would affect large numbers of ordinary users, compared with posts on small blogs or Internet forums, which could be blocked without the general population or the international public taking much notice. Interrupting a popular service can become an international news item and upset (and potentially politicize) formerly apathetic users, thus the social costs for governments often outweigh the benefits.

Valid arguments can be made against the use of large social media platforms. In particularly repressive societies, Facebook groups are the wrong place to organize political protest because of the public nature of this service. In Egypt, for example, activists achieved noticeable momentum for their protests in 2008, facilitated through Facebook—but the organizers were simply arrested by police, who could easily discover their plans. Activists, especially in authoritarian countries, need a degree of secrecy when organizing protests. Crabgrass, a noncommercial and open source social networking tool, allows for such a safe haven.

Despite its risks, Facebook can be valuable for activists if used with an awareness of the lack of privacy. While effective for ad hoc mobilization, public displays of political opinion on the social Web allow police or a secret service to readily map networks of dissent and to shut them down. As of the writing of this book, however, commercial platforms play an important role in most activist campaigns that make use of the Internet. As new social media are developed and begin to permeate the lives of those belonging to the global middle class, personal blogs and services such as Twitter and Facebook have become part of their daily routine and also their route into digital activism.

During the 2008–2009 Israel-Gaza conflict, Israel banned all journalists from the war zone; as a consequence, Facebook, Twitter, and YouTube became the global information frontline for this war. The war also played out on a dedicated discussion page on Wikipedia. Without intensive Web presence, Palestinians would have been absent from the international discussion about what was happening in Gaza. Both Israelis and Palestinians created Facebook applications that automatically replaced the status update of a given user with their political message. The Palestinian version notified people of incidents that led to the death of Palestinians, while the Israeli version generated alerts each time a rocket was launched against Israeli territory. More than seventy thousand users of Facebook installed "Qassam Count." In addition, the Israel Defense Forces created its own YouTube channel with daily reports by Israeli soldiers on the unfolding war. The information about the war in Gaza was channeled through social media.

Some noncommercial applications became very successful because they moved into a niche not filled by commercial applications. For example, the Kenyan advocacy software Ushahidi was used by Al Jazeera to allow Israelis and Palestinians to report protests, rocket attacks, casualties, and deaths, via Twitter and SMS. Ushahidi ("witness" in Swahili) places the submitted data on a Web-based map. Using the concept of "crowdsourcing" for political activism and public accountability, Ushahidi was first developed to map reports of violence in Kenya after the postelection fallout at the beginning of 2008. In 2009, Ushahidi was used to monitor the elections in India.

Conclusion

While the infrastructure of the Internet was first defined by struggles over protocols of the network itself, the commercialization of the Web in the mid-1990s led to more user-friendly services that allowed people to focus on content instead of having to concentrate on code. The public discussion moved from the network (protocols, ownership) to the tools and services that the Internet makes available. This chapter tracked the move from individual websites to customized templates, from small experiments with autonomy like Digitale Stad to political activism on large privately owned social utilities like Facebook.

Today, the Web is a highly centralized, commercial, winner-takes-all environment. Activists have realized that they can't just dream a better future into existence, they have to be present in the places where they can reach large numbers of people. New social media add to the activist repertoire and, while they are not by any means a magical solution to the complex problems facing today's activists, they can help to loosen the grip of repressive regimes. In fact, that's where they are most effective.

While this chapter acknowledges the possibilities of acts of digital activism on a corporate social networking service, we certainly should continue to support the building of sustainable, long-term, noncommercial infrastructures like the activist social networking site Crabgrass. The danger of overwhelming commercialism is that the resultant monoculture enforces digital cages on the Web—for example, choosing to leave (or never join) Facebook is a difficult decision because its millions of users make the service culturally powerful. The best environment for digital activists is a varied one, with many effective, accessible, and easy-to-use tools available.

Recall Tim Berners-Lee who reminds us that, through our actions, we are creating the Web. Some changes happen quickly on the Internet. The first part of this chapter covered 25 years, the last only 9. We must be mindful users and creators of the digital environments that we inhabit; together we are transforming the Web. This discussion about digital activism, its history, and usefulness often plays out in extremes. Either the Internet equals democracy, plain and simple, or activists are unambiguously helpless in the face of despotism despite the Internet. It is hard to find a thoughtful, historically informed mix of dystopian, analog, utopian, and techno-determinist takes on digital activism. But that is exactly what is needed.

Notes

1. Fred Turner, *From Counterculture to Cyberculture: Stewart Brand, the Whole Earth Network, and the Rise of Digital Utopianism* (Chicago: University of Chicago, 2006), 9.

2. Tim Berners-Lee, *Weaving the Web: The Original Design and the Ultimate Destiny of the World Wide Web* (New York: Collins Business, 2000), 86.

3. Geert Lovink, *Dark Fiber: Tracking Critical Internet Culture* (Cambridge, Mass.: MIT Press, 2003), 237.

4. Nicholas Carr, *The Big Switch: Rewiring the World, from Edison to Google* (W. W. Norton: New York, 2008), 110.

5. Berners-Lee, *Weaving the Web* , 2.

6. Berners-Lee, *Weaving the Web*, 57.

7. Reinde R. Rustema, "The Rise and Fall of DGS" (doctoral thesis, University of Amsterdam, October 8, 2008), http://reinder.rustema.nl/dds/ rise_and_fall_dds.html.

8. Dorothy Kidd, "The IMC: A New Model," *Journal of the World Association for Christian Communication* (2003. Web. 13 Jan. 2010. https://docs.indymedia.org/pub/Global/ImcEssayCollection/IMC_a_New_Model.pdf (accessed January 12, 2010).

9. Salem Pax, *Salam Pax: The Clandestine Diary of an Ordinary Iraqi* (New York: Grove, 2003). 137.

Applications: Picking the Right One in a Transient World

Dan Schultz and Andreas Jungherr

Introduction

The widespread adoption of online communication leads to social change, which offers the potential to bring about a major reshuffling of established power structures. Such realignment provides an unprecedented chance for political activists to gain influence for their causes.

All activism (and change) brings with it risks. One group of political activists might be able to use online communication effectively to organize collective action, while another might endanger its members and supporters through an easily traceable digital data trail. A group of activists might adopt a digital tool too early—before that tool gets widespread social traction—or successfully integrate a digital tool in the workflow of their organization and achieve a higher degree of efficiency only to have the tool discontinued a week later.

In this chapter, we discuss some of the issues that arise for activists when they adopt innovative technological tools. Since each group of political activists faces specific, individual challenges, we cannot deliver a blueprint of 10 neatly organized bullet points. Instead, we try to discuss some of the issues that activist groups will need to address when thinking about the adoption of innovative digital technology.

The Life of a Technology

When adopting any new technology, political activists face challenges that differ from the familiar challenges of activism. Instead of braving the rapids of political power brokering, mass media attention span surfing, and plain organizing, activists must become technologists—managing risk, paying attention to adoption trends, and deciding which opportunities to follow and which to leave behind.

In this section, we discuss two widely used concepts that are helpful when thinking about the life cycle of technologies. The first is the "Hype Cycle," a framework for analyzing the popularity of a technology; the second concept is adoption phases—the difference between early and late adopters—and their consequences for political activists who are trying to weigh the risks and benefits of incorporating a particular technology into their process.

THE HYPE CYCLE

The Hype Cycle is a concept that research and consultancy firm Gartner, Inc. developed in 1995 to analyze the adoption cycle of technologies. This concept has since has proven to be a valuable tool in understanding the popularity trends of new technologies.

The Hype Cycle helps companies and institutions with the decision about when to adopt a new technology by determining when the "buzz" around a new technology has died down. Since the adoption of new technology always incurs costs and a change in processes, any organization considering such investment wants to be certain that the technology can do what it claims and will have some staying power.

The Hype Cycle's Stages

1. **Technology Trigger:** Gartner's Hype Cycle begins with the launch of a new technology or product. If the new product's publicists have done their job, with some luck the product will steadily gain attention. Enough buzz might be generated to draw the notice of traditional media and established social networks. Early adopters will find splashes of success, driving up expectations and adding fuel to the fire.

2. **Peak of Inflated Expectations:** The next phase is a time during which the new technology or product is flying closest to the Sun, encountering and enjoying inflated expectations and over-enthusiasm but just about ready to face reality. Remember: Although the service or product is being overestimated doesn't mean it isn't useful. What haven't been discovered or mastered are best practices and the noise is at its highest point. Thus, the great majority of users and potential users are unable to make optimal use of the technological tool.

3. **Trough of Disillusionment:** As people realize that the new technology falls short of overblown expectations, the third phase of the Hype Cycle begins: The Trough of Disillusionment. Those who joined with unrealistic expectations will leave with numerous complaints, besmirching the brand as they do. Thus, a technology might suddenly become unfashionable and drop out of the tech reports "hot or nots."

4. **Slope of Enlightenment:** Afterward, what becomes possible is for the users who remain to experiment with the technology. A more realistic assessment, based on experience, of the technology's capabilities is possible. Groups and individuals now develop a better understanding of the technology's true benefits and risks.

5. **Plateau of Productivity:** The Plateau of Productivity is reached when best practices have been determined and a general ability to derive real value from the tool has been achieved—enough successes and failures have brought a general understanding of the possibilities among different use-cases. Widespread agreement on the pros and cons of a certain technology has been reached by both the general public and industry.

Political activists *must* understand the potential a technology holds before they commit to and base their organizational processes on a technology that might be short-lived or that will not serve their needs. Although the future can never be certain, the Hype Cycle is a valuable tool for analyzing the stage a technology has reached in its life cycle and enables those considering adopting a new technology to better understand its future potential.[1]

ADOPTION PHASES

For political activists, understanding the possible future developments of a new technology is important, but also important to understand is your audience and supporters. Different user types can be distinguished by their willingness to adopt new technologies. If the supporters of a given group of political activists consist mainly of early adopters, who jump on every new technological trend, the group might benefit from adopting new technologies quickly without too much thought about any long-term potential. If a supporter group consists mainly of those without access to technology or with a conservative attitude toward technological change, an activist group might be better advised to wait before adopting a new technology until it is adopted by the mainstream. As always, a one-size-fits-all solution does not exist; each group of activists must decide for themselves when they and a new technology are ready for each other.

Understand Your Options

Since so many choices are available when it comes to digital tools, you should spend a few minutes to understand some of your options, their benefits, and, equally important, what problems could arise.

SOME SANITY CHECKS

Don't panic; almost certainly a digital tool is out there that will help you do what you are trying to do. To have a good shot at finding (or properly using) that tool, you must understand your needs. We strongly suggest you think about these three questions:

- **What are your goals?** What are you hoping to accomplish with your organization? What are you hoping to accomplish with technology? Maybe you want to improve internal communication, drive recruitment, spread awareness of an issue, publicize events, or solicit support. There probably isn't a silver bullet for any of these tasks, but if you are not clear about them, then you're just wandering around in the dark.
- **How do things work now?** In many cases, incorporating technology into current practices is easier than completely reinventing your practices. Even if you are starting new or just want to start fresh, step back and look at the current state of affairs. Any practices that you definitely want to keep? Any you definitely want to change? Think of these potential requirements and ways that tools could fit in as you explore your options.
- **What resources are available to you?** You probably don't have a huge technology budget (if you have one at all); fortunately, time and money aren't the only useful resources. List out everything available to you: cause-friendly nerds you know, software you already own, computers, cell phones, iPods, whatever. Who knows what resources are out there that could help you take advantage of what you already have?

DECISIONS, DECISIONS

Deciding between specific sites and services will be much easier if you first understand some broader options—each one comes with its own problems and benefits.

"Hosting" or "3rd party"?

Hosting—setting up your own technologies on a server that you control directly or pay to control—isn't a trivial task. To host you need a techie, or someone willing to become a techie; creating and maintaining the service is more time consuming than just using someone else's—and, if something goes wrong, you are responsible for fixing problems.

Third party services, like Facebook or Twitter, are created, owned, and maintained by someone else. They were made with users in mind, so they should be usable; they were made with function in mind, so they should be functional; and, since they are on the Internet, their cost will range from $0 to a-million-times-cheaper than hosting it yourself. Furthermore, if you are using a popular or established service, you get to benefit from any network effects—a major plus for any social movement.

If hosting is such a terrible idea, why even consider it? One word: control. Hosting grants the ability to ensure that the system is up and running at critical moments and that information isn't censored or removed. Risk of the terms of service changing or the site inexplicably disappearing into thin air are nonexistent. If you have access to the code, you can also add features, change the look and feel, and customize it for your organization. In essence, hosting gives you the potential to have whatever you want, as long as you have the resources.

Hosting Pros

- You completely control the data and information.
- You can customize the service to best fit your needs.

Hosting Cons

- You're on your own if something goes wrong.
- Hosting is generally more costly than using free services.
- Hosting requires an extra degree of technological prowess (although you can probably find someone willing to donate time to your cause).

3rd Party Pros

- Sites you don't control have someone working on them to develop new features and generally improve the service.
- You have access to a preestablished user base.

3rd Party Cons

- You're at the mercy of someone else's maintenance schedule.
- Someone else controls the privacy of your information
- Whatever affects the 3rd party site affects you; when Twitter was hit with a DDoS attack, users were unable to access it, and when Facebook gets banned in Iran, so do you.

"Proprietary" or "Open Source"?

Is the system you'll use to support your movement owned by a private start-up? Is it the result of a collaborative open effort? These are actually trick questions because how the software came to be doesn't really matter, so long as it fits your budget and does what you want it to do. The availability of a support community and a strong sense of future development, however, are important, and that is where the production process can have a slight influence.

If you are going to dedicate time to adopting a technology, you care about a few things: How easy will it be to learn? Will it still be useful in the future? What can you change about it? A lot of the answers to these questions can be predicted by looking at the documentation and community chatter before you make a choice.

Support communities are a vital resource for everyone. They bring new functionality, best practices, answers to common questions, and the motivation to generally improve and keep things modern. Well-established, open source projects usually have great communities around them, which makes sense since the communities are what created them. Even proprietary systems can develop a raving support base; for instance, Facebook gives plenty of opportunity for expert users to add value through custom applications.

Another quality to consider is extensibility, i.e., the support for plug-ins and mods. By using a technology that allows others to add new features, you have a much better chance of being able to adapt to changing technical needs and trends. Open source projects are often designed to work this way, since the core product is probably an amalgamation of modules anyway, but proprietary systems also tend to provide ways to hook in through APIs and Web services.

"New Hotness" or "Old Reliable"?

You can easily get caught up in technology hype, and sometimes that isn't such a bad thing for an activist to do. Campaigns that use a new technology to accomplish something groundbreaking often end up generating positive attention for themselves. There is also no question that identifying and diving into what will become the next Facebook or Twitter would help you gain traction on the digital front. Using tools that are a bit further along the adoption curve, however, can have some real benefits.

Established systems have established networks, precedent, popularity, and brands. By using a brand that people recognize, trust, and use, you will increase your own credibility and remove some of the barriers to involvement in your campaign. If your intended use takes advantage of network benefits, then the larger user bases of popular sites are going to prove to be a vital asset. Even if the tool is going to be used for something private, like internal communication, you could find the robust support base that comes with established tools to be invaluable.

Another major blow against "cutting-edge" technology is the vast increase of added risk. The tool could disappear, it might be unstable, maybe its popularity is just a fad, maybe it just isn't going to grow any more—the list goes on. If longevity and stability are important for your purposes, you'll need to be careful before making commitments to a tool that has only been around for a year. If, however, you are OK with the risk of being forced to change directions at some point down the line, don't give this concern a second thought.

Of course, completely new isn't necessarily something to avoid. There will be times when new tools do something that nothing else can do or they are simply superior in the areas you care about. You should also recognize that even the most established tool could become obsolete in a week. What is important is that you know what you're getting yourself into and assess and address your risks accordingly.

"New Hotness" Pros

- If the service grows, you benefit as an early adopter.
- The tool might provide something new or improved.
- You might discover a groundbreaking way to perform digital activism.

"New Hotness" Cons

- It could fall flat, leaving you without an audience.
- It could die off completely, leaving you without a tool.
- It could change dramatically, possibly in a way that causes it to lose its original appeal.

"Old Reliable" Pros

- You probably aren't the first one trying to use the tool for activism, so there will be precedent and best practices to learn from.
- The larger user base provides network benefits.
- Established brand means others will be able to understand immediately how and why you are using the tool.

"Old Reliable" Cons

- Depending on your intent, you might have to fight for attention in an environment filled with noise from other causes.
- You might find yourself invested in an obsolete technology.

Know Your Risks

Technologies, like most things in life, don't come without risk. For many, the risk is barely worth thinking about—the worst that could happen is usually just minor inconvenience. For activists, however, a campaign is at stake. If the terms of service change, the site crashes or goes down for maintenance, or if the world moves to the next big thing just when you finally started to get the hang of the old one, trouble for the unprepared is often the result.

This section covers a few examples of risks you should be thinking about and a few mitigation tactics for those risks. The severity and likelihood of each risk and the effectiveness of the mitigation tactic will completely depend on your unique position and the technology, so it is up to you to apply it to yourself and come up with your own plan.

DATA RISKS

Lost Privacy—privacy online is difficult to maintain. Be assured that no matter how reliable and private you think a site's content might be, a way for the information to leak exists. This becomes a very serious issue when privacy is a prerequisite for safety. The best way to keep sensitive information private is to keep it offline in the first place. If that isn't possible, discuss the issue with a 3rd party administrator to understand the risks or host the information yourself on a technology you know is secure.

Lost Access—maybe the site went down temporarily or maybe content was removed from a 3rd party system by an administrator. Either way, you suddenly don't have access to the information. To avoid the problem, make sure you can send messages of high importance through multiple systems. For instance, instead of just posting on a Facebook wall, also set up an external site to display important announcements.

Lost Content—be it a hacker, a disk crash, or a bug in someone's code, content can unexpectedly disappear forever. For material you know you will need forever, back it up somewhere safe—maybe even in multiple places. If you think that backup will be a regular requirement, figure out a way to automate the process.

PROCESS RISKS

Changing Terms of Service—if you are using someone else's site and they change the terms of service, you might be left with terms you don't like. Try to get a feel for the culture of the tool before you start using it. Is it a corporation whose mission statement involves saving the world? Is it an open source project? If you want to be sure you won't find yourself between a rock and a hard place, make sure you have a backup plan if you ever need to make a fast switch.

Altered Features—the tool you are using may well change its feature set and remove the reason you wanted to use it in the first place. Pay attention to the buzz surrounding whatever you are using. Modern sites often have developer blogs with information about planned changes before they are implemented. If you are hosting your own software, just make sure you know what is in updates before installing them.

Unreliable Service—maybe a site is regularly taken down for maintenance or it is censored in certain parts of the world. If the downtime is regularly scheduled, learn its maintenance schedule ahead of time. If you think the downtime will be unacceptable or unpredictable, try to provide a secondary service for backup use.

TREND RISKS

Dwindling User Base—maybe something new is out there, or maybe people have just lost interest, but folks simply aren't participating anymore. Stay on top of technology trends and pay attention to what's popular and what isn't. If you think the technology you've invested in is on the way out, try to tie your current practices and services into the most promising new tools without sacrificing your existing infrastructure.

Failure to Take Off—you decided to be an early adopter or maybe you decided to host your own service; either way it turns out nobody is using it and nobody is participating in your campaign. Design your site/system so that even if the primary service fails miserably, you can fall back on a more reliable and popular secondary one. Continue to use both until the risk of failure decreases.

Conclusion

All of this might sound scary—it sort of is—but remember the countless examples of activists who were able to achieve amazing feats through cutting-edge technology and organizational processes. Their successes came about because somebody was courageous enough to experiment, even when that meant spending time hanging precariously by a thin technological thread. You get to learn from their precedent.

To further increase your chances of integrating technology with your daily routine in a way that goes beyond aimless tinkering and chance, here are a few final guidelines:

Remember the three questions: What are your goals? How do things work now? And what resources are available to you? To become successful in the adoption of new technology, first and foremost you have to ask the right questions. Without them you have little chance of finding a good solution.

Build redundancies: Remember that failures are inevitable. This is the way things work and there is nothing wrong with it. There is only one thing you can do about it: Build redundancies. Build a fail-safe. If a new technology fails, breaks down, or misbehaves, have something reliable ready to take over. Maybe that something is an old technology that would have gotten the job done but wasn't as attractive for some reason. What is important is that you have a process that ensures a reasonable solution in the case of catastrophe. Remember: There is nothing wrong with failure so long as you're prepared.

Keep trying new things: There is no silver bullet. Tools will change. Old ways of doing things will die with the technology they were built on. New ways will open up. There is no plan. No matter how long and deep you keep thinking about your procedures, in the end there will be no substitute for getting your hands dirty and building a prototype. Build it, and, if it works, they will come. If it doesn't work, scrap it. Throw your idea in the garbage bin of ideas and start anew. Keep trying, keep building, and keep tinkering.

Notes

1. For a more complete discussion of the Hype Cycle, its development, and its success, see the great book *Mastering the Hype Cycle: How to Choose the Right Innovation at the Right Time* (2008) by Jackie Fenn and Mark Raskino.

Devices: The Power of Mobile Phones

Brannon Cullum

The turn of the twenty-first century has seen the rise of mobile phones as powerful devices that have transformed how people create and share information. Organizations and activists are harnessing the power of mobile technologies to improve and expand campaigns, better coordinate activities and demonstrations, and increase awareness about social issues. Activists, armed with either low-cost, basic mobile handsets or more complex smart phones, are capable of instantly connecting with their network of colleagues and supporters.

Economic and Demographic Argument for Mobile Phones as an Important Tool for Activism

These days, mobile phones are pervasive not only in the industrialized world but also in developing countries, making them an appealing tool to activists. In early 2009, the United Nations' International Telecommunications Union estimated that 4.1 billion people worldwide subscribed to mobile phones. Two-thirds of these subscribers were in developing countries. Moreover, mobile use is growing most quickly in sub-Saharan Africa, the Middle East, and Southeast Asia.

Mobile phones are often the most effective mode of communication across the world. People can often more easily access and own a mobile phone than a personal computer or a landline. Not only is mobile often cheaper, but many countries still lack the basic infrastructure to support the use of the Internet. Fixed Internet access in many developing countries is still limited in some areas and can be prohibitively expensive. In addition, an Internet connection may be slow, thus using a mobile device may be a quicker way to reach someone—which is appealing to activists who may need to have ready and reliable communication with others.

Reductions in the cost of owning and using mobile phones have made it easier for activists to use them as tools. While costs and pricing structures vary from country to country, in general, costs have been decreasing over the past decade. In most countries, cost-effective "pay as you go" plans with a mobile provider are the norm. These prepaid plans have helped increase the penetration of mobile devices because potential users do not have to undergo credit checks, sign contracts, or pay monthly bills. Users also commonly have multiple SIM cards in order to get the best rates. (A subscriber identity module [SIM] is a small, removable card in a cellular phone used to identify subscribers to mobile and data networks.) Savvy mobile phone users can purchase multiple SIM cards and swap the cards out to get the best rate at a particular location or time or to avoid potential surveillance from aggressive regimes.

Activists who have the financial means to purchase a more expensive smart phone—a mobile phone that has many of the functions of a personal computer—have benefited from its advanced capabilities by being able to do more than just sending text messages. DigiActive's 2009 report on digital activism noted that survey participants who had mobile phones with more features were more likely to use their phones for activism. Gartner, Inc., a leading information technology research firm, estimated that worldwide sales of smart phones in 2009 was 179 million, up from 139.3 million devices sold in 2008. The firm further predicts that sales will reach an estimated 525 million units in 2012. (While the study indicates that the majority of sales are in North America and Europe, sales are slowly increasing in developing countries.)

Characteristics of Mobiles for Activism

Both the portability and pervasiveness of mobile phones make them appealing to individual activists and advocacy groups. While many simply use mobile phones for communicating with friends and family members, activists have seized upon what scholar Raul Pertierra calls "the unexpected social potency" of the devices and have created new ways of communicating and engaging in social practices.

These new modes of participation have heightened individuals' relationships to one another and to their governments. In his 2002 paper, "Little Boxes, Glocalization, and Networked Individualism," University of Toronto sociology professor Barry Wellman asserts, "In networked societies, boundaries are more permeable, interactions are with diverse others, linkages switch between multiple networks, and hierarchies are both flatter and more complexly structured."[1] It has become easier and cheaper for individuals to actively engage in civil society.

The widespread adoption of mobile phones has given rise to what Wellman refers to as "networked individualism." People are still connected to one another, but the individual is less rooted to a geographic area and can easily switch between and among social networks. While telephones have traditionally facilitated one-to-one communication, mobile phones provide the additional possibility of communicating indirectly from one to many. Such ability is certainly useful when trying to coordinate activities among a group of people who may or may not know one another.

The use of mobile phones supports both top-down, hierarchical structures as well as looser person-to-person communications.

During the 2004 Orange Revolution in Ukraine, residents of Kiev spent more than two weeks protesting the results of the presidential election, which they believed to be fraudulent. To increase the effectiveness of the protest, Pora, a pro-democracy group that spearheaded the effort, used short message service (SMS), or text messages, to coordinate demonstration shifts and disseminate information among participants. Working from the top of the organization down, Pora's leaders employed SMS to schedule shifts that moved people between nearby makeshift tent cities and the city's central square to prolong the demonstration. The protests resulted in new, legitimate elections that brought opposition candidate Viktor Yushchenko to power.

In the absence of organizers, independent actors can use applications and tools on mobile devices to cooperate and coordinate in ways that were previously impossible. The individual has more autonomy when in possession of a mobile phone, yet unique partnerships also evolve as people work together using new technologies to achieve collective goals. When users cooperate with one another, they also build trust, enabling collective action on a larger scale. In 2007, one million people in Xiamen, China, gathered to protest the building of a proposed toxic chemical plant. Many Chinese learned about the protest via a text message warning them of the dangers of the plant, asking people to participate in the protest, and to forward the message. Officials in Xiamen abruptly suspended plans to construct the plant because of the wave of opposition and public denunciation of the project.

Information that is shared within a social network can radiate out rapidly. Using mobile technology, a joke, rumor, political message, or link can spread contagiously, like an epidemic. When a person forwards a text message with instructions or information to those in his phone's address book, it is received by individuals who personally know and trust the sender. If the receiver believes the message to be true and important, he or she likely will then forward the message to others. The message will then spread beyond the original dense network into a wider, more loosely connected network. When messages start spreading virally, authorities have greater difficulty halting their spread. Examples abound of political jokes being disseminated via SMS to generate awareness of the indiscretions of political leaders. In 2006, Iran erupted in uproar after Pres. Mahmoud Ahmadinejad was one of many Iranians who received a joke via text message saying he didn't bathe enough. Ahmadinejad was incensed by the anonymous text, feeling that the insult undermined his position as Iran's leader. He had many people arrested because he believed they had been involved with the joke and fired the president of the state's mobile phone company that carried the message. In July 2009, the Pakistani government began an investigation into SMS jokes circulating about Pres. Asif Ali Zardari and threatened to arrest and jail anyone who sent such messages.

Mobile phones are also ideal for activism because communication can be maintained even when the mainstream media are cut off. Many individuals who previously relied on mass media channels to share information are now able to more actively participate in the public sphere using mobile devices and other social media tools. Rather than relying on official reports to relay news, average citizens can take on some of the responsibilities previously shouldered only by journalists. During the 2007 protests in Burma, the government banned most foreign media outlets and outlawed reporting against its policies or actions. Many civilians, however, were able to share news with friends and the press using text messages and uploading photos and videos to the Web. Pakistani citizens engaged in similar actions in late 2007 and early 2008 when the country was under emergency rule and the government shut down or censored independent electronic media outlets. Civilians used their mobile phones to alert radio stations about events; the stations then rebroadcast these accounts as public announcements.

Mobile Applications and Platforms Used for Activism

In recent years, activists have experimented with various mobile applications and tools to support their causes. Tools such as SMS and photos have become fairly standard on even the most basic phones. New technologies and applications, such as Twitter, global positioning systems (GPS), and downloadable ringtones, are available on a growing number of mobile phones, thus further expanding the power of mobile activists to effect change.

SMS

The use of SMS is central to mobile activism, in part because the price of sending text messages is low enough in most countries that it is rarely an impediment to subscribers. Texting has become a common communication tool in many developing countries where making voice calls remains prohibitively expensive. Using SMS is also more efficient and less time-consuming than making a voice call.

Activists have used SMS in a variety of innovative ways, including to recruit supporters, share information, and facilitate the movement of people before and during a demonstration. In 2006, the Republican National Committee (RNC) encouraged people to become supporters by texting "JOIN" to a specific short code— a phone number with fewer numbers than a regular telephone number, making it easier to remember. These supporters would later receive text message updates from the RNC about campaign efforts. During the 2008 U.S. presidential election, organizers for Barack Obama integrated SMS into their overall campaign strategy as well. They effectively conducted a successful campaign by texting supporters to make announcements, share reminders to vote, and promote speeches. Among the many official and unofficial efforts to encourage citizens to vote in the 2008 U.S. presidential elections, YrMama4Obama (http://yrmama4obama.com) called on individuals of voting age as well as children under 18 to text the organization and get text updates about why you should vote for Obama. The body of the texts asked receivers to pass the message on to everyone they knew.

Many organizations have also experimented with petition signing and fund-raising via SMS, where users typically text a short code and their name to a specific number as a show of support. In 2004, Fahamu, a South African and U.K.-based nonprofit that aims to aid social justice movements in Africa, set up a text message petition campaign to support the ratification of the Protocol to the African Charter on Human and Peoples' Rights on the Rights of Women in Africa. Although a Web-based petition was already gathering signatures, Fahamu set up a system whereby users could sign the petition via SMS, with their signatures then appearing on the online petition page. In the eyes of the organization's leaders, the campaign was a success. Out of four thousand signatures collected, some five hundred originated in text messages. Similarly, during a series of concerts held in 2005 for the ONE Campaign to fight poverty and AIDS, U2 lead singer Bono asked fans to send texts with their names to a specific number as a show of support. The names were then displayed on a giant screen on stage. The organizers later used these phone numbers to share news about future campaign efforts.

BULK TEXT MESSAGING

New developments in SMS service have enabled mobile phone users to send bulk text messages—a very useful strategy for advocacy organizations seeking to send a unified message or pertinent information to supporters. These services can reach large numbers of people much more quickly than other mechanisms, like electronic mailing lists, that require an Internet connection. Two of the most widely used platforms are TxtMob and FrontlineSMS. TxtMob was first used by protesters at the U.S. Democratic and Republican national conventions in 2004 to warn about the location of police, to direct volunteer medics, and to coordinate the movements of participants more efficiently and in real time.

While bulk messaging services can be useful and efficient, they do have limitations. To receive bulk messages, users typically must sign up for the service online and verify ownership of their mobile phones. These requirements may prevent many from using the service because they may not want to go through the hassle of signing up or to share their personal information with an untrusted service. Also, many may be less likely to respond to a message, forward it to others in their network, or follow instructions if it comes from someone outside their direct, personal network.

VIDEO AND PHOTO

One powerful method activists and protesters use to garner attention is sharing of video and photographs captured on mobile phones. Nowadays, most cell phones have a built-in camera, and many also support video. YouTube enables registered users to upload videos from their phone directly to a YouTube account. User-generated content can easily be shared not only with contacts but also with local and international media outlets, thus quickly reaching millions worldwide.

In September 2007, images and videos disseminated via mobile phones showed the world Burma's military junta violently repressing antigovernment protests by Buddhist monks. The government had attempted to present only a sanitized version of the demonstrations, repressing any news about violence. Nevertheless, foreign media outlets, many of which the government prevented from reporting inside the country's borders, were able to share news of the events because they had access to transmissions from citizen journalists. Similarly disseminated were the June 2009 opposition rallies and protests in Tehran and other major Iranian cities that followed the presidential elections. Many Iranian citizens alleged that the election results were fraudulent and took to the streets demanding a recount. With news media, including Al Jazeera and BBC World, claiming that the Iranian government was censoring broadcasts and jamming signals, many outside of Iran learned about the protests from violent images captured on cell phones and beamed worldwide.

RINGTONES

Another tactic many advocacy organizations use to raise awareness about causes is to offer downloadable ringtones on their websites. Having a ringtone that is related to a particular social or political campaign enables individuals to show their support of, and solidarity with, an issue. The Center for Biological Diversity, based in New Mexico, offers the sounds of endangered species (rareearthtones.org) to raise awareness about the issue. As part of a 2008 campaign to fight the spread of HIV in India and promote socially responsible behavior, the BBC World Trust offered a ringtone aimed at breaking down the social taboo of using a condom. To promote the "condom a cappella" ringtone, the Trust produced a funny commercial in which the mobile phone of a man attending a wedding goes off blaring, "Condom! Condom!" The commercial directs viewers to a website (www.condomcondom.org) to download a similar ringtone.

TWITTER

Activists are increasingly using Twitter, a free micro-blogging service, to share information, coordinate activities, and organize movements during an event. Twitter allows people to communicate by posting short messages, up to 140 characters, to their news feeds. Users can send and receive Twitter feeds through their computers, mobile applications, or SMS, and also choose other users whose feeds they would like to follow. The Twitter platform provides a search function where users can search using keywords and hashtags. For example, those interested in seeing if any users were tweeting about protests at the G20 summit could search "#G20" or "#G20protest."

Since users can update Twitter via their mobile phones, postings can increase the number of people within a loose social network who can be made aware of coordination efforts or news alerts. Live tweeting enables a person to share her message with people beyond the contact list in her mobile phone. In addition, activists can use postings on Twitter to gain the attention of traditional media outlets.

Groups of activists can also use Twitter to track each other's movements. When American student James Karl Buck and his translator were arrested during antigovernment protests in Egypt in April 2008, Buck was able to send a SMS to update his Twitter feed with the word "Arrested." Buck's friends following him on Twitter then secured his release within hours.

Despite increasing use, Twitter has limitations. One problem is that Twitter only works in areas with mobile coverage. During demonstrations in Moldova in April 2009, the protest site had little to no coverage, so participants couldn't access Twitter. Twitter may prove a better platform for information sharing and preparation, rather than real-time coordination of efforts if the government can shut down network coverage during an event. As Twitter becomes widespread, more governments and law enforcement groups are using it and regularly monitor the platform for information.

Other micro-blogging platforms, including Plurk, Identi.ca, and Jaiku, are an alternative to Twitter, but activists use them infrequently because they are less popular with the general public.

LOCATION-AWARE APPLICATIONS AND NETWORKS

New location-aware applications for smart phones have had tremendous success in the arena of citizen journalism, crisis reporting, and election monitoring. These applications use the built-in GPS sensors in mobile phones to pinpoint a physical location.

During 2008 postelection turmoil in Kenya and 2009 violence in Gaza, citizens reported the exact location of incidents using SMS and their phones' GPS.

Recent innovations include location-based social networks and platforms such as FourSquare, Brightkite, Loopt, and Google Latitude. These types of applications permit mobile phone users to transmit their precise location and could potentially be of great use for tracking and coordinating movements as they occur. For example, instead of someone texting to find the location of a friend at a demonstration, he could find that person via a map on the Brightkite platform. Because of the limited availability (many location-based software applications only work on certain higher-end models of smart phones) of these applications, however, activists have not widely adopted them. As these phones are expensive, such applications are unlikely to become pervasive in the immediate future.

Tactics Used for Activism

Social activists currently use several tactics enhanced by mobile technology. While each has its limitations, combined, they have enabled organizations and individual activists to successfully institute practices of smart mobbing, election monitoring, reporting, and *sousveillance* for social good.

SMART MOBBING

Forming a smart mob is one of the most common forms of mobile activism. The term was coined by scholar Howard Rheingold in *Smart Mobs: The Next Social Revolution* (2002). A smart mob is a group of people who cooperate and coordinate their actions primarily through the use of mobile phones, PDAs (Personal Digital Assistant), and SMS. Smart mobs usually lack centralized control, although sometimes activist groups will be primarily responsible for guiding their formation. Those who make up a smart mob often do not to know one another.

The 1999 protests at the World Trade Organization meetings in Seattle were one of the first times activists used mobile phones. Activists formed a smart mob by using mobile phones to coordinate their movements and evade police. The protesters were able to function as a group because they relied upon SMS to receive information on where to go and what to do.

ELECTION MONITORING AND OBSERVATION

Mobile phones have been critical in combating voting fraud, monitoring elections, and countering rumors in both developed and developing countries. Katrin Verclas, cofounder and editor of MobileActive.org, a global network of practitioners using mobile phones for social impact, notes that mobile phones are being used in two different ways in elections: a more informal, citizen-generated and crowd-sourced election monitoring and data collection; and a systematic, organized monitoring that trained volunteers undertake using a strict methodology. Both groups have benefited from mobile technology as it provides them with a quick way to record and report information and results. Formal and informal mobile election monitoring has taken place in a number of countries, including Ghana, Kenya, Mexico, India, Lebanon, and Sierra Leone. The U.S.-based National Democratic Institute for International Affairs (NDI) created a simple SMS-based system that is frequently used to monitor elections and report irregularities. NDI has been a key player in training volunteers worldwide to participate in systematic, organized, data-based monitoring.

Former United Nations secretary general Kofi Annan applauds the use of mobile phones in ensuring free and fair elections. He stated to CNN on August 25, 2008, "With communication and cell phones, this is where it is difficult to cheat in elections now. You are announced at the district level and cell phones go wild so by the time you go to the capital, if you have changed the figures, they will know and you will be caught out."

Using SMS, participants can share information about vote counts and any irregularities. Democratic activists hope that through increased civilian and independent media participation, the election process will be more transparent and accurate.

Sharing stories, video, and photographs can provide evidence to support more formal observations. However, relying solely on the work of crowds would be ill-advised. As Ian Schuler of the National Democratic Institute, who has written extensively about the role of mobile phones in election monitoring, points out, informal citizen monitors don't have the ability to officially verify and report information on election counting and results.

CITIZEN REPORTING AND DOCUMENTATION

Another tactic used in mobile activism has been sending texts to report incidences of violence, human rights violations, and abuse. One of the most well-known cases was when Ushahidi, an open source platform, was used to amass reports of violence following the 2008 elections in Kenya. Citizens submitted text or email reports to the organization, which then plotted incidents on a map on its website. Using the same open source tools, Al Jazeera launched a similar site in January 2009 for citizens in Gaza to report incidences of violence, disruption of daily events, or abuse. Al Jazeera then mapped reports from its own journalists and public contributors. The primary challenge when using crisis-reporting platforms is that the information provided might not always be accurate and credible.

"SOUSVEILLANCE"

The growth in applications available for mobile devices also increases the potential for average citizens to actively monitor government, law enforcement, and corporate action. Corruption, police brutality, and corporate crime have become harder to conceal since anyone with a mobile has the power to play watchdog. Steven Mann, a professor at the University of Toronto, coined the term "*sousveillance*" to describe what he called "watchful vigilance from underneath"—the recording of an event or activity from the perspective of the average observer. Ethan Zuckerman, a fellow at Harvard's Berkman Center, refers to *sousveillance* as "the monitoring of authority figures by grassroots groups, using the technologies and techniques of surveillance." Unlike citizen reporters who may happen upon an event, those engaging in *sousveillance* are acting with the specific intention of capturing potentially illegal or immoral activity. On January 1, 2009, multiple mobile phones captured video of an Oakland, California, police officer shooting Oscar Grant, a young, unarmed man, who was being restrained by other officers on a rail platform. The mobile videos were uploaded to sites like YouTube and Witness.org. The footage spread virally across the Internet, and, after viewing, many members of the public organized rallies. Grant died of his injuries; the officer was ultimately charged with murder.

International Case Studies

PEOPLE POWER II, THE PHILIPPINES (JANUARY 2001)

One of the most successful and widely known uses of mobile phones for activism was the organization of protests, known as the Second People Power Revolution (People Power II), to topple Philippine president Joseph "Erap" Estrada in 2001.

President Estrada was brought to trial in the Senate on charges of corruption and mismanagement in December 2000. He had already become increasingly unpopular amongst Filipinos; sending anti-Estrada text messages, mainly in the form of jokes, was commonplace. When television news broadcasts announced that 11 senators had voted against unsealing evidence that would have easily convicted Estrada, the public was outraged. Filipinos immediately began texting one another to organize protests demanding Estrada's resignation. In 2002, one year after People Power II, mobile phone subscribers numbered 11 million—out of a population of 78 million. At that time, Internet penetration was less than 1 percent and landline density was 3 percent. Thus, in the revolution, the mobile phone quickly became the key tool in coordinating collective action.

On receiving text message instructions to gather in protest, many Filipinos flooded the streets of Manila. Typical SMS messages included:

> The 11 senators are pigs! S&@t, Estrada is acquitted! Let's do People Power! Pls. pass. . .

> WEAR BLACK TO MOURN THE DEATH OF DEMOCRACY.

> Military needs to see 1 million at rally tomorrow, Jan. 19, to make a decision to go against Erap! Please pass this on. . .

Demonstrations and protests were held over five days, with an estimated one million Filipinos participating. Eventually, Cabinet members fled their posts, police and army personnel sided with the protesters, Estrada resigned, and Gloria Arroyo was sworn in as the new president.

The text messages that led to the mass demonstrations were not the result of an SMS alert system where Filipinos had signed up to receive texts about emergencies or calls to action. Rather, Filipinos received messages from individuals within their existing social networks. The origin of the first messages calling for a gathering at the site of the 1986 revolution (People Power I) is unknown. However, it is not a stretch of the imagination to think that multiple individuals had the same idea to organize at the same place as they did 15 years earlier.

Without the text messages that were sent shortly after the televised announcement of the Senate's vote, Filipinos would not have been capable of coordinating their actions on such a large scale so quickly. A crowd could have been mobilized via voice messages, emails, and word of mouth. Low Internet penetration, combined with the time-consuming nature of calling each person within individual social networks, however, would have prevented the demonstrations from occurring quickly. Smart Communications, Inc., a mobile operator in Philippines, reported that in one day, more than 70 million text messages were sent (the daily average was between 30 and 40 million). In contrast, an online petition calling for Estrada's resignation hoped to collect one million signatures, but received only 91,000.

The events of People Power II illustrate how conditions ripe for political action, coupled with the power of emerging mobile technology, can combine to create a powerful movement with lasting consequences. The public combined its outrage with collective action, and it proved successful.

PARLIAMENTARY ELECTIONS, SPAIN (MARCH 2004)

The use of mobile phones during the 2004 general elections in Spain illustrates how ordinary citizens can shift the direction of an election. On March 11, 2004, days before national parliamentary elections, three trains were bombed at a Madrid train station, killing 192 people and injuring hundreds more. In the immediate aftermath of the bombing and before any evidence had surfaced linking any specific terrorist organization to the event, the governing Popular Party (PP) publicly stated that the Basque terrorist group ETA was behind the bombing. By the end of the day, the Islamist terrorist organization Al Qaeda had claimed responsibility for the act. The Spanish government, known for taking a hard stance against the Basque group, continued to assert that ETA was culpable, in part because making the Basque terrorists appear responsible would benefit PP in the upcoming elections against the Socialist Party. Many Spaniards were outraged that the government was choosing to blame Basque terrorists for Al Qaeda's work and believed that the PP was trying to cover up evidence that linked Al Qaeda to the bombings. Opposition leaders believed that Al Qaeda targeted Spain because of Prime Minister Jose Maria Aznar's support of the war in Iraq and that Aznar was downplaying the role of Al Qaeda in an effort to improve his party's chance in the election. Citizens, agitated by the apparent manipulation of information, began to call for demonstrations to express their mistrust of the government.

According to blogger Andre Serranho, the first SMS message was sent March 13, the day before the election, and simply stated, "The government lied. Pass it on." Other messages soon began circulating, such as:

> 18:00 PP head office Genova St. no parties silence for the truth.

> Information poisoning at 18:00 PP Genova pass it on.

> We want to know before we vote.

> The truth now, stop the manipulation, your war, our dead. Pass it on!

No one has been able to identify the source(s) of the texts. The Socialist Party has vehemently denied responsibility. Spain has an official ban on political demonstrations in the 24 hours prior to any election. Activists and concerned citizens ignored the ban and gathered anyway. By 11:00 p.m., more than ten thousand people had gathered in front of the PP headquarters in Madrid.

In Serranho's account of what transpired on March 13 and 14, he notes that the majority of Spaniards he spoke to acknowledged that they had forwarded text messages to their contact lists. Spain had a mobile penetration rate of 94 percent, indicating that most residents of the country had mobile phones capable of sending and receiving texts; March 13 saw a 20 percent increase in text messages, March 14, election day, saw a rise of 40 percent. Thousands of texts were passed around asking Spaniards to vote for the Socialist Party and to demonstrate against the Popular Party.

These tactics proved successful. The large size of the group that gathered at PP headquarters showed how many people were upset with the incumbent party. In a surprising turn, the Socialist Party defeated the PP at the polls, with turnout for the election estimated at 77 percent—an 8 percent increase from the previous election.

Thus was demonstrated the power of persuasive text messages. It can be posited that many Spaniards who received text messages trusted the sender enough to believe the accusation against the government and decided that the best way to protest was to vote for the opposition party.

ENVIRONMENTAL ADVOCACY, GREENPEACE ARGENTINA

Greenpeace Argentina has done an impressive job of integrating mobile technologies into its strategic operations in novel, and often successful, ways. In 2005, the organization experimented with a mobile phone campaign as it lobbied for a "Zero Waste" law in Buenos Aires. This law called for a reduction in the amount of waste going to landfills. Greenpeace Argentina supporters received text messages from the group asking them to call legislators and lobby for the passage of the law. One text read (translated): "URGENT: call right now to the legislator Jorge Giorno to 4338-3028/3215 and ask him to approve Zero Waste's Law. We count on your help." Texts were also sent to coordinate demonstrations and share urgent news. The Zero Waste law was ultimately passed in late 2005.

In 2007, the organization replicated these tactics on a larger scale. In an effort to combat rapid deforestation in Argentina and to gain support for the passage of *La Ley de Bosques* (the Forest Law), Greenpeace Argentina harnessed many forms of media to reach the public and engage supporters nationwide. Again, text messages played an essential role in the campaign.

La Ley de Bosques would provide a one-year moratorium on the clearing of old growth forests in Argentina, as well as authorize the establishment of public hearings and environmental impact studies. To gain backing for the legislation, Greenpeace Argentina asked its supporters to sign a petition on the organization's website and to provide an email address and phone number. Greenpeace Argentina then assembled a database of more than three hundred fifty thousand mobile phone numbers.

Supporters were then contacted via text message with the latest news on the legislation and action alerts—short texts asking supporters to complete a simple action such as calling specific legislators to lobby for the passage of the law. Hernan Pablo Nadal, Greenpeace Argentina's online organizer, recalls that at one point constituents were making up to three hundred calls per hour to legislators. The campaign proved successful, and the Forest Law was passed in 2007.

The organization has also used mobile technologies to empower indigenous communities in Argentina. In 2004 and 2005, the government wanted to auction off a part of the Pizarro Reserve, a nature reserve in northwestern Argentina. Conservationists and the indigenous Wichi people who lived on the reserve were active in protesting the government's actions.

Greenpeace Argentina equipped the Wichi with mobile phones and instructed them to send text messages whenever they saw developers clearing the reserve's land. Activists alerted via these texts then went to the reserve and chained themselves to bulldozers. Greenpeace also used SMS to mobilize supporters to participate in demonstrations and rallies. Ultimately, the campaign was successful.

One of the key lessons Greenpeace learned about coordinating a successful advocacy campaign was to send out text messages only at strategic intervals, such as during the lead-up to legislative deliberations on the law, instead of inundating its supporters with multiple texts. If texts were sent too frequently, users grew tired or annoyed. The combination of a large, active database of supporters and the strategic sending of text messages has enabled Greenpeace Argentina to win significant legislative victories. While firm figures are hard to establish, the organization reported that 15 to 25 percent of its *móvil activistas* have given feedback stating that they actively took part in a particular text message-based campaign.

The Challenges of Mobile Activism

The primary challenges of using mobile phones for activism include barriers to use and the fear of government surveillance. While many people across the world may find accessing a mobile phone easier than getting on the Internet, developing countries still have areas where cost and coverage are a hindrance. In industrialized and developing countries alike, governments are becoming savvier in their methods of tracking mobile activists, creating anxiety among many.

BARRIERS TO USE

Cost and lack of coverage are primary factors in the reluctance of advocacy organizations to use mobile technologies. Obviously, most organizations aim for making the maximum impact at the minimum cost. Unfortunately, the cost of purchasing, setting up, and maintaining mobile devices can be significant. Some mobile service providers do offer cheaper fees for nongovernmental organizations, however.

While infrastructure to support the use of mobiles in rural and underserved locations is growing, and mobile coverage is often easier to put in place than is an Internet connection, many areas in developed and developing countries still have no service available. In addition, in some areas with unreliable or limited hours of electricity, charging a mobile phone may be difficult. The United Nations, the World Bank, and the Global Social for Mobile Communications Association (GSMA) have each spearheaded initiatives to reduce the cost of owning and operating a mobile phone. These campaigns will help to put mobile phones in the hands of low-income activists; for example, the GSMA's Mobile Broadband initiatives focus on developing a ubiquitous mobile broadband infrastructure. The organization's Development Fund works to increase the delivery of mobile phones to the world's poorest people.

SECURITY CONCERNS AND GOVERNMENT INTERVENTION

Those participating in advocacy campaigns and activism often worry that their activities on mobile devices are being monitored and traced; they are often also concerned that the government might intervene to hinder their work. Closed platforms for mobile devices, where the control of software development is held firmly by the device manufacturers and is not available to software developers for experimentation, pose the greatest threat to activists who wish to operate below the government's radar. Since the code is closed, users cannot determine whether or not their phones have surveillance features. Open platforms enable software developers to read the code and build precautions into the software and operating systems to avoid surveillance and thus assuage the fear of traceability. Guardian is a project that aims to build an open source smart phone distribution using Google's Android software to ensure that users can communicate safely and securely. Advances in open source will enable activists to independently produce and deliver information with greater privacy.

Governments have reacted to citizen demonstrations and protests primarily by blocking SMS transmissions or by shutting down mobile networks intermittently or in particular locations. For example, following contested elections, the Ethiopian government banned SMS from 2005 to 2007. The king of Nepal took similar steps in 2006, after democracy advocates organized protests. The government of Iran also shut down SMS during the demonstrations that followed the June 2009 election. Banning SMS usually takes the cooperation of telecommunications operators, who typically are unwilling to shut down the service and lose revenue. In Ethiopia and Nepal, however, telecom operations were owned by the state. Anticipating government actions is difficult, and activists who rely on mobiles have limited options if a network is shut down.

Governments have also begun copying the strategies of activists. For example, during 2005 protests in China against the ascension of Japan to the United Nations Security Council, the Chinese government used mass texting to warn its citizens against participating in opposition activities. As governments attempt to catch up with the technology and tactics activists use, they will increase their use of SMS and other ways of communicating with citizens via mobile phones. The effectiveness of nongovernmental organizations and the abilities of citizens to run and participate in advocacy campaigns and activism can be improved if activists and others get training to develop their skills and knowledge of various applications, platforms, and devices. Activists should strive to stay at the front of the learning curve by experimenting with the latest mobile security and privacy tools.

The Future of Mobile Activism

As smart phones become more affordable and more developing countries shift to 3G mobile networks, new applications, platforms, and software will transform how individuals and groups engage in activism. In May 2009, Nokia announced that it intended to offer smart phones at a lower price to reach more consumers. The following month, Apple slashed the price of its base-level iPhone from $199 to $99.

While many activists will continue to coordinate their actions by using text messages, others will take advantage of the variety of applications becoming available to make organizing easier and more efficient. While not abandoning traditional methods, many organizations and activists are using advanced mobile technologies to enhance their campaigns.

Governments and nongovernmental organizations have been working to close the digital divide—the gap between those connected and those not connected—and to make mobile technologies more affordable. The International Telecommunications Union has made it a priority to connect all African cities and villages by 2015—including boosting mobile coverage and broadband penetration and making a commitment to infrastructure development. Throughout the developing world, moves to deregulate state telecom monopolies continue. By opening up mobile phone providers to competition, citizens will benefit from a reduction in cost and the breaking of government monopoly in the telecom market. A 2009 study by the *International Journal of Electronic Security and Digital Forensics* suggests that the rapid growth in the use of mobile phones is helping to close the digital divide.

Innovative initiatives undertaken by various organizations and individuals worldwide will also continue to empower activists. For example, kiwanja.net, founded by Ken Banks to help nonprofits use mobile technologies in innovative ways, launched the Mobility Project (mobility.kiwanja.net/), which works to enhance the mobile phone code-writing skills of application developers in Africa. Just as FrontlineSMS, TxtMob, and Ushahidi pioneered the successful creation of mobile applications for activists, this new community of programmers is expected to develop equally innovative programs.

It cannot be emphasized enough that mobile phones are simply tools that can supplement the work of activists but not replace them. What really matters is how the tool is *used* in the hands of average citizens, activists, and organization leaders. As more and more social advocates and activists become armed with mobile phones and take advantage of mobile technologies, the evolution of the use of mobile phones to advance social causes and campaigns will continue apace.

Notes
1. B. Wellman, "Little Boxes, Glocalization, and Networked Individualism" in *Digital Cities II: Computational and Sociological Approaches*, ed. M. Tanable, P. van den Besselaar, and T. Ishida, (Berlin: Springer-Verlag, 2002), 10–25.

Economic and Social Factors: The Digital (Activism) Divide

Katharine Brodock

As Internet use became a worldwide phenomenon in the 1990s, much attention was given to the disparities in access among users. Collectively, these disparities were labeled the "digital divide." Originally, the term was used to call attention to the differences in availability of computers, and then to access to the Internet. It has since expanded to refer to the more conceptual issues of technological expertise, socioeconomic status, and cultural influences. The Organization for Economic Co-operation and Development, an international organization of 30 countries that accept the principles of representative democracy and free market economy, currently defines the digital divide as "the gap between individuals, households, businesses and geographic areas at different socio-economic levels with regard to both their opportunities to access information and communication technologies (ICTs) and to their use of the Internet for a wide variety of activities."

While digital activism promises to increase the effectiveness of grassroots efforts around the world, the digital divide hinders this process by limiting participation. In discussing the digital divide and how it can be overcome, the first step is to identify how the divide manifests itself with regard to activism. In this chapter, we will discuss three principal manifestations of the divide: unequal access, unequal skills, and, briefly, censorship.

In a way, these three can be seen as a continuum. Access is the most basic indicator of digital technology use and refers to the infrastructure of digital communication, which can mean either access to an end device, like a mobile phone, or a network that connects those devices, like the Internet. Research shows that patterns of technology access often mirror, rather than undermine, traditional power dynamics, which at times challenges the vision of digital technology as a political equalizer.

Once access to infrastructure is gained, use of that infrastructure is made via software applications, which could be anything from an email client to a social network or word processor. Even those who have access to infrastructure may not possess the skills needed to operate the applications that make that piece of infrastructure useful. Broken down into its component parts, digital activism can be seen as the effective execution of a series of technological skills carried out to achieve a strategic goal. Thus, inequality of skills can have a significant effect on activist outcomes.

Finally, even if individuals and groups have both access to infrastructure and the skills necessary to manipulate applications, they may still be prevented from using these tools if their government chooses to censor or block a given technology. Several governments have decided to block digital technologies for a variety of reasons, many of them political—thus, significantly limiting the options of activists.

By analyzing the digital divide at these three levels, we will explore why certain people are more likely to become digital activists than others and look at possible solutions. The greatest promise of digital activism is that it will serve as a foundation for a more equal and participatory political system—one in which all individuals have the opportunity and ability to speak, assemble, and coordinate more easily through the use of digital technologies. If certain citizens are unable to participate, then this promise is difficult to fulfill. For this reason, we study the divide's effect on activism; we seek to understand it in order to overcome it.

Access

Access to digital tools is one of the initial and greatest hurdles to closing the digital divide. More digital technology, including computers, mobile phones, handhelds, etc., and more connection capabilities—Internet, broadband, optical fibers networks, etc.— must be provided and made accessible to the world's underserved populations, the argument goes.

Those who point to problems of access as the main cause of the digital divide maintain that providing these tools to greater numbers of people will result in users reaping the benefits of digital technologies and that the digital divide will begin to narrow. Governments and organizations hoping to decrease the digital divide in their own countries or regions often have access to digital technology as one of their main agenda items. The Internet Society, an international nonprofit founded in 1992, works very closely with many developing countries to "enhance the availability and utility of the Internet on the widest possible scale." It also provides leadership in Internet-related standards, education, and policy. The organization has placed enabling access at the top of its list of goals.

EMPOWERING EXISTING ELITES

Research indicates that economic differences limit not only access to technology but also the likelihood of an individual to take part in political activism. The 2009 Digital Activism Survey conducted by DigiActive, an organization dedicated to helping grassroots activists around the world use digital technology, found that digital activists, particularly in developing countries, are more likely than the population at large to be paying a monthly fee for home Internet access, to be able to afford a high-speed connection, and to work in a white-collar job with access to the Internet in the workplace. In short, digital activists are likely to be prosperous, with their economic resources offering them a significant digital benefit. These initial findings indicate that the digital divide strongly influences digital activism because it tends to limit participation to the economic elite.

This research was corroborated by a report of the Internet and American Life Project of the Pew Research Center. A September 2009 Pew report—"Civic Engagement Online: Politics as Usual," by Aaron Smith—stated that "whether they take place on the Internet or off, traditional political activities remain the domain of those with high levels of income and education." Smith continues: "Contrary to the hopes of some advocates, the Internet is not changing the socio-economic character of civic engagement in the United States. Just as in offline civic life, the well-to-do and well-educated are more likely than those less well off to participate in online political activities."

The digital divide is also made wider by the fact that not only do lower-income populations have less access to digital technologies, they sometimes must pay more for them. For example, the 2007 ITU-UNCTAD World Information Society report stated that the cost of broadband as a percentage of the average monthly per capita wage was around 2 percent in high-income countries, whereas broadband costs in low-income countries were more than 900 percent of the average monthly per capita wage. Higher-income populations are not only likely to receive the higher-quality products of modern communications technology and in greater supply, they often are able to purchase them at significantly lower relative cost.

Combined with the research on digital activism participants from DigiActive and the Pew Research Center, these findings indicate that digital technology often mirrors rather than undermines preexisting divides in economic resources. Digital technology provides new communication capacities, but it is people of higher economic capabilities who are best able to take advantage of them.

A REFLECTION OF OFFLINE SOCIAL INEQUALITY

While access to digital technologies is incredibly important and is actively championed by many as a "solution" to the world's myriad problems—in our case, as a way to effect political or social change—in many ways, the digital divide is not a digital problem. Rather, it is the digital manifestation of offline social and economic inequality.

ICT-for-development pioneer Nancy Hafkin surmises that unequal access to technology by men and women in some countries hinges on cultural practices. At a talk at Harvard's Berkman Center for Internet and Society in 2006, she noted that "access to technology isn't gender neutral—there's a complex set of factors that make it less likely that women will get access to technology." For instance, "In most developing nations, access to the Internet is from public centers, not from the home. . . . Because of the poor reputation of cyber cafés, parents discourage girls from going. . . ." In a case in a Ugandan school, documented by the women's technology group WOUGNET, "seats in a computer lab were given to the students who arrived first. The boys ran from the classroom to get seats, but the girls—who'd been trained to be polite and ladylike—walked and didn't get a single seat." Thus, cultural ideas—both simple and complex—about gender roles can affect who gets access to technology and also who can be a digital activist.

India's social networking landscape offers another example. One of the most popular social networks, Orkut, closely mirrors the Indian caste system that has been in place for millennia. For instance, even within the same social network, the communities for high-caste Brahmins are almost completely separate and divided from the communities for the "untouchable" Dalit caste. In addition, research by blogger and social media entrepreneur Gaurav Mishra has shown that, as of June 2009, Orkut had one thousand Brahmin groups, whereas it had only two hundred groups for and by members of the Dalit caste. "Perhaps, the low number of Dalit communities on Orkut says something about Indian society in general, and Orkut users in particular," Mishra remarks on his blog at Gauravonomics.com. "Higher, more powerful, castes like Brahmins, Rajputs and Yadavs tend to have more money and easier access to the Internet and old disparities are further accentuated by the Internet."

Just as the DigiActive report indicated that digital activism was an activity of the economic elite, these examples show that social barriers may also carry over into the digital realm—challenging the hope that digital activism can be an equalizer for socially and economically marginalized groups. Although we might hope that digital activism will engage new voices in political causes, it may also simply provide a more effective means of advocacy for those who already have a relatively privileged position in society.

When existing elites are most able to take advantage of digital tools, what does that mean politically? In an international context, it means that citizens of higher-income countries sometimes use digital tools on behalf of the world's poorest peoples. For example, the online Save Darfur campaign attracted the attention and support of American celebrities, including George Clooney and Don Cheadle. Some may argue that such developed world activism reinforces colonial power dynamics—the areas receiving the benefits of these efforts become beholden to the societies supporting them—or that the solutions to a problem are then dependent on the likely inaccurate, though well-meaning, perceptions of the "giving" society or individual. On the other hand, those who have the access and skills to use digital tools for an effort such as Save Durfur are initiating the campaign and, in some cases, offering the only opportunity for these causes to have a voice online.

CLOSING THE GAP THROUGH LEAPFROGGING

Is there a way for people who are not privileged to gain access to the technologies of digital activism? Yes, and that process has been termed "leapfrogging." Leapfrogging is the idea that poor countries can skip over stages in technology adoption—especially large-scale, industrial, infrastructure-heavy technologies—and implement newer and more efficient technologies that are lightweight, distributed, and ecologically sustainable.

One commonly cited example is mobile phone usage. Although we mostly think of leapfrogging as occurring in developing countries, it also occurs in developed ones, which have internal digital divides and technologically disadvantaged populations. A 2009 report by the Internet and American Life Project contained some interesting statistics on mobile phone usage as a possible effort to leapfrog expensive computer set-ups as a way to access the Internet. The report showed recent growth in Internet-enabled mobile devices to be most significant among African Americans, a group that experiences poverty in higher percentages than the American population at large.

The *New York Times*, reporting on the data, stated that "the percentage of African-Americans using mobile phones or another type of connected gadget to share e-mail, exchange instant messages and access the Internet for information on an average day has more than doubled since late 2007, jumping to 29%," compared with 28 percent of whites. John Horrigan of the Pew Internet Project says that, "the cost of broadband and personal computers drives some users to adopt mobile Internet instead of the traditional wire-line." In America, as in much of the world, individuals and families who may not be able to afford to buy a computer are leapfrogging to Internet access via a lighter and cheaper mobile device.

Mobile phones may prove to be a very important digital tool for much of the world's lower-income populations. In 2009, the United Nations' International Telecommunications Union (ITU) estimated that two-thirds of the world's 4.1 billion mobile phone subscribers lived in developing countries. Mobile phones have been used for digital activism in countries as varied as the Philippines and Belarus. As mobile phones decrease the access gap, they also decrease the digital political participation gap. What remains to be seen is how much other limits on digital activism, such as the cultural factors identified by Gaurav Mishra and Nancy Hafkin, will affect participation rates as access to mobile digital technologies rises.

Skills

While many of the arguments for increased access are compelling, what happens when people actually do get access to digital technologies? Will they know how to look for information on the Net using a search engine? Will they know how to connect to others online, whether by sending an email, signing an online petition, or starting a group on a social network? These are legitimate questions for all activists who wish to expand the reach and power of digital technologies. Those who believe that having access to digital technology is not enough to close the digital divide point out that an individual, group, or organization must know how to use the technologies to take full advantage of them as activists. It is for this reason that we now focus on the digital divide of skills.

A TAXONOMY FOR DIGITAL SKILLS

Eszter Hargittai, an associate professor in the communication studies department of Northwestern University, has focused much of her research of the past several years on this issue of access versus skill. She has found that while improving universal access to broadband is necessary, it is not sufficient for achieving a knowledgeable and engaged Internet citizenry. Her acronym—UBER GEM—lists the skills necessary for effective use of digital technology:

U: Understanding what's possible
B: Being able to perform the function
E: Engaging effectively & efficiently
R: Recognizing privacy, security, and legal issues

G: Getting assistance

E: Evaluating the credibility of material

M: Managing the material

Many people lack a cognitive map of what's available online and thus may not be able to filter and manage what is. Questions that may be asked to judge the skill level of a user include: Do you know what tools are available to help you complete a given task? Do you know how to conduct a thorough search? Do you know how to join an email listserv? How careful are you with spam messages? Do you understand your legal rights? Where is your information coming from?

Many people assume that everyone who has access to Internet services is using them and that everyone who has an Internet service is participating and sharing on the variety of interactive platforms available through today's "read-write Web." But those who are commenting are the ones engaged—and this is a minority. According to the 90:9:1 rule, on a site in which all users are permitted to create content, only 1 percent will be heavy contributors, 9 percent will contribute occasionally, and 90 percent will consume content without contributing. While personal preferences are certainly at work here, skills are also important. A large percentage of the online population, especially those fairly new to the Net, simply doesn't know how to engage in these online activities.

STRATEGY AS A SKILL

Once we move beyond the issue of gaining the skills needed to navigate digital technologies, a marked divide remains between those who know how to use these tools and those who know how to build a strategy around them. The use of technology in the 2009 post-election protests in Iran offers an interesting example of the effects of different technical skill sets. Although from the outside it appeared that opposition elements in Iran were quite strong, such impression may simply have been made because they were more effective at broadcasting their message than were the more conservative citizens who supported the current regime. Those in Iran who opposed the official outcome of the election and supported change seem to have had greater digital access and skills than those who supported the government.

In a post on the international citizen media site Global Voices, blogger Hamid Tehrani suggested that part of the high-profile and seeming success of protesters was attributable to their demographics, as protesters (for the most part) had more knowledge of digital technologies than the more conservative forces supporting the president. These protesters were more able to get their message out effectively, through tools like Twitter and YouTube, than were the faction that supported the current regime. Protesters also had the combination of skills and strategic insight to use English to broadcast news of the antigovernment protests to an international audience. The voices of the tech-savvy young protesters were most clearly heard in the digital medium, which reaches significantly greater numbers worldwide than do older media formats and rose above the noise of less effective new media tactics.

In the past few years, the number of organizations around the world attempting to use blogs, Twitter, and social networks to promote their causes has increased significantly. Some succeed while others fail. Even for organizations that have equal access to technologies and have members with the basic skills needed to create an account and post content, there exists a great disparity in their ability to use these tools strategically in a way that helps the organization achieve its goals. Capacity to use a tool as it was designed does not imply the ability to use a tool for activist purposes. Although new tools are ever more user-friendly, a learning curve exists—users must move quickly along if they are to transfer from basic functionality to successful campaigning. Few ever achieve such level of expertise.

SITUATING SKILLS WITHIN CULTURE

To some extent, the infrastructure of the Internet also plays a part in widening the digital divide. The infrastructure and protocols of the Internet were established and then refined in a particular culture and are thus imbued with the values in which these systems were created. Although we like to think of the Internet as rationally defined and culturally neutral, it is reflective of the specific worldview of those who created it and the cultures that they were a part of.

In his book, *Technology and Social Power*, Graeme Kirkpatrick of the University of Manchester calls this the "politics of design." In any device, the "innards" that the creators have designed to make the device function—memory, processor, modem—exist within a "black box" that is invisible and incomprehensible to most users. The machine functions by projecting messages on a screen that forms the environment in which the user can interact with the device. Says Kirkpatrick: " . . . part of technology design is precisely making clear to the user what they [*sic*] can or cannot do with it."

The Internet has a politics of design—a set of assumptions about efficiency and use in the minds of its architects. As an example, the algorithms in place for search queries are based on an assumed user behavior of how people would go about looking for various pieces of information online. These assumptions were based not only on scientific ideas of computer engineering and usage, but also on the cultural and personal expectations and desires of those architects, conscious or not.

Censorship

So far we have looked at unintentional causes of the digital divide in activism: access hindered or helped by economic and cultural factors and unequal skills. However, sometimes governments step in to intentionally divide the digital universe for political reasons.

Online censorship creates a wall between certain populations and their ability to gain access to and use digital tools for activism.

According to the OpenNet Initiative, a joint research project of four leading universities in North America and the United Kingdom, the number of countries that limit access to the Internet has increased rapidly in recent years. The organization's website notes that:

> Drawing on arguments that are often powerful and compelling such as "securing intellectual property rights," "protecting national security," "preserving cultural norms and religious values," and "shielding children from pornography and exploitation," many states are implementing extensive filtering practices to curb the perceived lawlessness of the medium.

Censorship can take a number of forms, from blocking access to certain websites or services to filtration of search terms, removal of undesirable content from accessible sites, and encouragement of self-censorship through intimidation and persecution of activists. China, which has the world's most pervasive filtering practices, has blocked, for instance, both Twitter and Facebook on numerous occasions, probably because of those sites' ability to facilitate communication and coordination outside of government control. Digital censorship is not limited to the Internet. A white paper by the organization MobileActive.org contains research by blogger Ethan Zuckerman, who notes that the governments of Iran, Albania, Nepal, Thailand, and Cambodia have all blocked the use of SMS (short message service) in the periods before elections.

Unlike the digital divides involving access and skills, censorship attempts to control the content available to the population as a whole. While the privileged are more likely to have the skills necessary to access blocked sites and applications, it is not specifically because of their socioeconomic position that they have access while others do not. With the ability to evade censorship—the knowledge of circumvention technologies like TOR, UltraSurf, Psiphon, and proxy servers—the digital divide also becomes a skills divide. In addition to divides created by lack of access and insufficient skills, direct blocks on digital tools limit the ability and capacity of digital activists to send and receive information and to coordinate actions.

Why the Digital Divide Matters for Activism

The digital divide threatens to impede digital activism by limiting participation to a group with more access to digital tools and greater technological experience and skills. As a result, while the capacities of digital tools profoundly expand the capacity of activists to communicate and organize, these tools lie in the hands of a relatively small number of people, challenging the perceived capacity of digital technology to upend existing hierarchies. Offline social dynamics and economic position are often carried over into online spaces. Cultural practices and socioeconomic segregation can go unnoticed, which can act to increase the divide and make it more difficult to close.

Furthermore, while access may be necessary to begin to close the gap, it is not, in itself, sufficient. Computer skills and concepts are incredibly important to the discussion of the digital divide— not only the skills necessary to navigate the Internet, but also the ability to develop a deeper-level strategy and successfully implement campaigns for change.

Last, while the digital divide is for the most part a result of unintentional socioeconomic, cultural, and experiential circumstances, in some cases the digital divide is intentional. Censorship contributes to the digital divide because it cuts off many of the world's people from access to the most powerful communication and mobilization tools.

By addressing each of these issues, we can begin to identify the problems that impede digital activism as well as determine how to slow the expansion of, or even begin to narrow, the digital divide. If the digital divide begins to close, more activists will be able to utilize digital technologies in their work and advocacy efforts, thus beginning to realize the greatest potential of digital activism.

Political Factors: Digital Activism in Closed and Open Societies

Tom Glaisyer

> "Six people. Ten minutes for creativity and action. A few hours of information on networks, Facebook, blogs, SMS to friends, and an e-mail newsletter. All of the organization through the Internet. On the street came out 15,000 young people! . . . Only the young, and no [political] parties."[1]
>
> —Natalia Morar, Moldova

Such descriptions of digital activism, often breathlessly picked up by foreign media, seem *de rigueur* these days when a protest challenging an authoritarian government occurs. However, such reporting is often followed by commentary that suggests that the story is a little more complex. Months pass, and the narrative is often reversed, key activists have been jailed, political momentum has been lost, and those with most to gain from the protest are said to be estranged from the much-heralded technology. Nevertheless, those who have worked at the center of power are still enamored of the possibilities. At the September 2009 Gov 2.0 conference in Washington, D.C., John Podesta, former chief of staff to Pres. Bill Clinton, said he considered emerging communications technology as a "tool of empowerment," referring to its use by citizens in societies where political expression is constrained. At the same conference, Carl Malamud, an early Internet pioneer, proclaimed, "we are now witnessing a third wave of change—an

Internet wave—where the underpinnings and machinery of government are used not only by bureaucrats and civil servants, but by the people."

The apparent contradictions between experiences on the ground and the conference comments above require further analysis of what happens when activism and governance become intertwined. Understanding how governments, policy makers outside of government, and the new digital movements interact is the focus of this chapter. It suggests that the paths in open and democratic societies will differ substantially from those in countries where governments repress dissent. Paths forward are likely to be many and stability a rare commodity as societies and governments adopt tools and practices at varying paces.

Two Cautions

First, we should refrain from drawing too much from any one of the very small number of cases that have played out at a national level to date. The cases do provide some insight into how activism occurs, but to suggest that they collectively reveal anything more than a partial range of possibilities would be drawing stronger conclusions than I believe are warranted. The history of social movements is complex and diverse, and the use of digital tools connected by an ever-more-extensive digital network is only the latest innovation in an ever-expanding repertoire of action.

Second, we must recognize the complex prerequisites involved in embracing the practices and tools that underpin movement-like digital modes of production—of which Wikipedia continues to be the exemplar. In January 2001, many believed it was improbable to have an encyclopedia written and edited entirely by hundreds of volunteers. Today, Wikipedia harnesses the labors of more than 140,000 individuals in any 30-day period. What is often ignored in the story of Wikipedia are its failed precursors—Rick Gates's Interpedia first described in 1993 and Richard Stallman's

GNUPedia, first described 1999 but only begun in 2001 at approximately the same time as Wikipedia.

Although clearly the ability of the World Wide Web to offer encyclopedic knowledge has been proven, we have to consider that we may be at a point in the history of digital activism that parallels Wikipedia's situation in 2001 or 2002. Technological challenges and the lesser reach of the Internet in the 1990s that limited the possibilities of earlier crowd-sourced encyclopedias could be said to parallel current constraints on the effectiveness of today's organizing tools. The reach of any particular tool is unclear, and though billions are now connected in ways they weren't before and could participate, in practice only a relatively cosmopolitan digital elite manipulate the tools with ease, as the chapter on the digital activism divide discussed in greater detail.

Bear these caveats in mind as we analyze how digital activism has brushed up against governments of all stripes.

Repressive Authoritarian Societies Counter Digital Activism

Many repressive and authoritarian governments have seen digital activism appear and gather momentum quickly. Although only a few have succeeded in effectively preventing any meaningful access to digital communications tools, activism in most cases has been less consequential than at first expected. The Moldovan case mentioned earlier, inconsequential as it turned out to be in the end, arose in a matter of days—as did the April 6 strike movement organized in 2008 in Egypt with the help of Facebook. Both of these movements can be critiqued as standing on weak, narrow, or shallow foundations, but the history of the movement that arose around the disputed elections in Iran in 2009 suggests that even those efforts that build on a base of significant social support are repressible.

In an article addressing the Egyptian protests, David Faris, a political scientist who specializes in the Middle East, relates that digital technology provided several opportunities for control that exceeded the methods employed to constrain purely offline organizing. Device registration and tracking (both of mobile phones and USB [universal serial bus] wireless modems for laptops) became more sophisticated. As a result, text messages were more routinely blocked, and Internet café user registration was implemented through new restrictive regulations. All in all, the technological dimension of the movement, particularly with respect to devices that are easy to track (mobile phones, for example), provided more opportunities for comprehensive surveillance than had the tools not been used.

Because of the intentionally opaque nature of political surveillance in Egypt, knowing the full extent of digital surveillance is impossible—though the success of state authorities in identifying and imprisoning key digital activists gives strong evidence that at least some digital surveillance was done. Regardless of actual surveillance practices, the fear that these capabilities instill in would-be activists creates a chilling effect that is often enough to lessen the willingness of activists to use technology. Furthermore, whatever the number and content of communications, they may be blocked or the users may be tracked, leading activists to lose faith in the ability of technology to perform at key moments or to reach the maximum audience and to abandon messaging systems out of fear.

The history of the Iranian protests in 2009 followed a similar path. In this case, Twitter was highlighted in the international press as the technology that enabled the protests to spread quickly, though the reality appears to be that news of protests was spread quickly because the sheer pervasiveness of various digital platforms sustained via multiple networks and communications devices. Comparison can be made to the Iranian protests of 1979 when the shah was overthrown. The distribution of sermons via tape cassette is said to have played a major role as did synchronized prayer on the rooftops of Tehran's houses, all of which led to massive protests similar to those 30 years later.

In 2009, the protest grew quickly, praying was repeated, but the cassettes were replaced by SMS (short message service), blogs, Twitter, Facebook, and email. Undoubtedly such tools enabled faster transmission of messages and quick-to-gather "flashmob"-type protests. Nevertheless, it appears that, in a manner similar to Egypt in 2008, state authorities used a variety of methods to delay communications—temporarily switching off mobile phone communications, intercepting SMS messages, and choking off communications between the country and the outside world. Subsequently, authorities have become more subtle and have merely slowed access speed to the Internet at key moments, thus making it difficult for the average user of the Web to surf for very long or use anything but the simplest and most basic Web applications.

However, perhaps the most significant innovation of the Iranian authorities was to use the same tools the protestors used to map and understand the relationships between protestors. By merely requesting that those passing through immigration on their return to Iran log into Facebook, authorities easily garnered information on the networks of relationships that would have taken months to painstakingly understand prior to the digital age. Even more cleverly, it has been alleged that the Iranian intelligence services have created fake accounts using the names of prominent dissidents to gain the trust of dissidents' friends and subsequently harvest data from friend networks. As reported in the *Wall Street Journal* in December 2009, harassment extended to families of Iranian expatriates who had been targeted as a result of Twitter posts by the expatriates.

In China, a country that has more Internet users than any other country in the world and is well known for filtering the Web, authorities have been even bolder. Not only have they used the tools of activists, they have also empowered counter-activists. They have built on the vigilante efforts of individuals engaged in so-called Human Flesh Search, training them, as described in greater detail in the chapter on destructive activism, and subsequently financing these individuals to defend Chinese state interests. These paid Web activists, known as "Red Vests" or colloquially as the "Fifty Cent Party" because they receive 50 Chinese cents per action, amplify the official version of events, post pro-government comments on social media platforms as well as report users who have written comments critical of the official line.

The Chinese government has apparently fully absorbed the significance of what individuals networked together via the Internet can achieve; it is suppressing the digital activism of its adversaries by using the same digital tools its opposition relies on. Such use of the digitally enabled counter-activist is perhaps the logical end point for digital activism in repressive regimes that permit (or are unable to completely suppress) the use of such tools.

Governments and Digital Activists in Open, Democratic Societies

The accounts of digital activism in societies that are open and democratic are more hopeful. Such activism is potentially more expansive. As well as raising challenges to current leaders, activism can also play a role in electing governments. Digital activists can also potentially participate in policy formation, execution, and monitoring, often in partnership with governments.

ACTIVITIES ELECTING AND CONTESTING GOVERNMENT

In 2009, a digital campaign in the United Kingdom aimed to expose the alleged dumping of poisonous waste in Côte d'Ivoire by the Swiss company Trafigura. In that case, the posting of an internal report on the transparency site Wikileaks and the re-tweeting of the URL by activists on Twitter, which newspapers in the United Kingdom couldn't do as a result of an injunction, undermined the efforts by Trafigura to keep the matter secret. Thus, the legal injunction became meaningless because information about the alleged actions circulated widely.

Journalist and digital activism commentator Evgeny Morozov, often pessimistic about the possibilities of digital activism, sums up the different outcomes possible in open and closed societies in his assessment of the case. In his blog, "Net Effects," Morozov writes:

> The reason why the anti-Trafigura campaign succeeded is that the U.K. already enjoys a rather healthy democracy, whatever its minor shortcomings are. A similar campaign in Belarus or Uzbekistan would almost surely fail, because state newspapers have nothing to lose . . . , the private sector doesn't exist, and bureaucrats do not really care about their reputations. . . .

The preeminent example of digital activism and electoral politics in an open society comes from the United States—the 2008 Barack Obama presidential campaign that embraced practices of digital activism on a large scale. It has since become the standard against which digital activism in service of an election is measured. The tools were critical to the mobilization of thousands of individuals—partly because the technology lowered the cost of activating, motivating, and managing the participation of large numbers of supporters.

Moreover, the technologies and practices used in 2008 by Obama for America, which were, for the most part, built on what was learned from the failed Howard Dean campaign in 2004, are now beginning to be used by Obama's opponents. The conservative "tea party" movement, which through grassroots efforts is forming the core of uncompromising opposition to President Obama's legislative agenda, is gaining adherents through electronically mediated groups of grassroots activists.[2] Such efforts, though they are becoming an ever-more-central component to any open and democratic election, have no role in countries with sham elections. The authenticity inherent in election-related digital activism, though useful to democratic political actors, has little value to an autocratic government.

Digital Activism in Government

Delving a little more deeply into the potential of digital activism in open societies, we consider the possibility of activists and government working together. Even in open societies, government organizations are considered the archetype of hierarchical bureaucracies: praised when successful in achieving seemingly impossible logistical feats such as the *Apollo* Moon landings, but more often derided as inefficient, expensive, and corruptible. Carl Malamud's earlier statement about how the Internet makes the machinery of government accessible to the people speaks to something profound. Let us take a moment to reexamine policy-making processes, how government is organized, and, specifically, the opening of government to the digital activist.

For example, parts of the U.S. government are clearly embracing these new possibilities. Vivek Kundra, chief information officer of the federal government, and Aneesh Chopra, chief technology officer and part of the Office of Science and Technology Policy (OSTP), are leading the information transformation under way in the U.S. federal government. The OSTP has been at the forefront of a three-stage process to construct policies around transparency, participation, and collaboration. It did so in a manner that permitted ordinary citizens to post questions, with later stages allowing for filtered, on-topic discussions, and the collaborative drafting of proposals. All of these activities appear to have provided legitimacy and meaningful input for the subsequent internal policy-making process.

In this way, both activists and ordinary citizens were able to directly voice their opinions about open government policy and have a say in its outcome, not through lobbying and private meetings, but through formal channels newly created to bring citizens into government. That said, such early steps do not a revolution in policy formulation make.

Another ongoing change suggests a more widespread, long-term change for activists outside government in setting policy. Transparency initiatives independent of specific policy objectives are becoming more common. Digitally stored data are easy to share outside government. Examples include initiatives such as Data.gov, a portal that provides raw feeds of machine-readable data; USAspending.gov, which is a portal into the federal government's technology expenditures; and the recently relaunched Recovery.gov, which seeks to provide transparency on spending associated with the American Recovery and Reinvestment Act of 2009 (which was designed to stimulate the economy following the recession of 2007–2009).

Skeptics could dismiss those who overstate the transformative effects of this new age of transparency, and, realistically, we must ask exactly how many people are going to contrast and compare (or "mashup" as the new terminology goes) Wyoming's Toxics Release Inventory with Medicare Cost Reports and identify a public health issue that a government employee has not. Moreover, the likelihood is that few have the skills necessary to do this kind of data analysis, thus, we believe, little of consequence will occur in the short run.

Nonetheless, these recent initiatives provide value not just in the data they release, but in the fact that they offer the ever-present possibility of someone discovering a public policy problem or, in the case of expenditures, evidence of corruption. What's important is not that everyone has time to do the analysis but the fact that it could be done. The reality that proof of overspending can be seen alongside other indicators of performance failure might have a disciplining effect on those charged with implementing policies or spending tax dollars. All of this is supplemented by organizations such as the Sunlight Foundation, which has challenged software developers to code tools to enable simple oversight. One such tool is Data Masher, which permits users to combine published datasets, another is ThisWeKnow, which summarizes datasets into digestible chunks. Needless to say, all these efforts provide solid evidence of activists hoping to hold their government to account.

This embrace of digital tools extends to foreign affairs. The Department of Defense co-opted efforts of digitally savvy young officers who had created tools to collaborate and had developed Company Command and XO.com. Both became popular as a result of a need to iterate responses to evolution of insurgent tactics in Iraq in 2003 and 2004. The State Department has developed Diplopedia and the intelligence community has set up Intellipedia to facilitate collaboration within their respective agencies.

Perhaps one of the most surprising movements to emerge is GovLoop, a social network of 20,000 people who work in government. GovLoop sprung up around the enthusiasm of Steve Ressler, formerly an employee of the federal government; he created a vibrant online "Facebook for government" where people he describes as "government innovators" can get to know one another and collaborate outside of their roles and normal circles. Now that bureaucrats have the ability to collaborate and organize outside of the office, we may see movements for reform developing within the government.

Internationally, similar developments have occurred in other democratic countries. In the United Kingdom, innovation led by MySociety.org has resulted in the development of several tools that assist activists. The most significant has been a petitions site on the Prime Minister's 10 Downing Street website that permits anyone to start or sign a petition. Other tools available to U.K. citizens include a site called TheyWorkForYou.com, which provides easy searchability of records, and WriteToThem.com, which provides a platform for sending messages to members of Parliament.

A number of initiatives are under way in South America. In Chile, Felipe Heusser has formed an organization, Vota Inteligente, that is dedicated to bringing transparency to the politics of the country via a website that aids accountability by comparing the political platforms and promises of the candidates, as well as the level of transparency candidates have with respect to their candidacy. In Brazil, CongressoAberto has been built with a similar mission—it tracks the votes of members of Parliament, the status of bills, and the amount and source of campaign donations.

Elsewhere similar efforts, though small, are occurring. In Kenya, Mzalendo, an online resource, has the simple objective to keep the Kenyan citizenry informed. Focused on the Kenyan Parliament, it aims to open up Parliament and demonstrate that demanding accountability from public institutions is possible. It lists contact details for members of Parliament and basic information on the progress of bills through the legislature. In Jordan, until recently Ishki.com, a site dedicated to receiving complaints from citizens, gave voice to those who otherwise would have none. It also permitted users to create petitions and ask others to sign them, request help from others, and also to praise or thank a person for an action taken. This leads to the question: How can the responses of governments best be differentiated?

Where This Might Lead: Open, Agnostic, and Closed Governments React

The responses of governments will likely follow one of several paths. Some governments will fail to adapt in any way and continue to operate as bureaucratic hierarchies despite the challenge from networked movements. Others will choose to follow an adaptive approach as a result of the success of their newly networked opponents and incorporate peer-to-peer practices. Such adaptation in open societies, as described above, might accommodate oppositional movements as it has in the United States.

Closed, authoritarian societies like Iran or China, on the other hand, will, in all likelihood, adapt to digital technology by using it to repress opposition movements. The disposition of the government toward digital activism will be significant in defining the impact that this kind of activism has on a society.

OPEN GOVERNANCE

In societies where political leaders and state institutions understand both the power of digital activism and the opportunity it presents for doing tasks differently, digital activists will likely be able to play a significant role as the structures of governance change. Such governments will embed digital networks of contention and cooperation into their operations, seeking to engage cooperative networks externally and recognizing oppositional networks as they arise as legitimate actors. In this context, governments and activists will likely learn the new dynamics and the political system will tend to move through the transition with the least amount of upheaval.

AGNOSTIC GOVERNANCE

Democratic governments that fail to recognize the emergence of digital activism, its possibilities, and the threat to established institutions will likely misunderstand any activism that occurs. Activists will find themselves in opposition and underappreciated. More than likely, such governments will misjudge the power of nascent movements and accede to their demands when unnecessary and refuse to compromise when it is in their interest. The transition to a world where digital activism plays a role in governance will be bumpy, as traditionally strong institutions are challenged and the concept that activists can play a supportive role will be unacknowledged.

CLOSED AUTHORITARIAN GOVERNANCE

Where open dissent is unwelcome, digital activism will almost certainly be repressed. In a few cases, governments will succeed in both tightly limiting access to digital platforms and in squashing dissent through traditional means. Where digital activism is at all possible, a contest between surveillance and countersurveillance technologies will ensue. In the bleakest case, the tools of digital activism will be used to enlarge government control over the population and likely result in less freedom.

Conclusion

In the short run, digital activists, who often have few options when opposing governments, tend to exploit technology more quickly than those they challenge, who are constrained by bureaucratic decision-making structures. Whether, in the long run, power will shift from repressive governments to activists is unclear. An argument can be made that as long as the Internet is open and permits people to connect using ever-changing technology, its infrastructure will favor those who can adapt quickly. What also must be recognized is that, to date, digital activism has not been completely eliminated in any state where it has been able to gain a foothold.

However, stepping back from the passion and energy of the activists involved, we must be skeptical and temper our expectations, being careful not to mistake novelty for political transformation. Flashmobs in the squares of capitals that don't normally see protest, asking questions of a sitting president over the Web, and editing policy documents online are redolent of the same novelty that "click here to send a message to your congressperson" had in 1999, courtesy of MoveOn.org, or that fax-centric advocacy did earlier in the 1990s.

In many ways, this activity just replicates earlier periods where advances in communications technologies permitted political contention. The printing press is said to have unleashed a hundred years of instability across Europe in the fifteenth century, while the rise of newspapers in the nineteenth century was heralded as ushering in a new era of access to political information. In the twentieth century, radio and television changed how politics and governance operated by introducing a truly mass media. In addition, the fax machine and email were crucial at key points in the 1990s, including in treaty negotiations. If digital technology is nearly as transformative as Malamud or Podesta suggest, we need to hold on tight and expect a bumpy ride.

Notes

1. http://www.rferl.org/content/Moldovas_Twitter_Activist_Under_House_Arrest/1610122.html (accessed February 15, 2010).

2. See http://www.reteaparty.com/teaparties/ and http://teapartypatriots.org/Groups.aspx (accessed February 14, 2010) to observe the breadth of the activism.

PART 2

Practices: Digital Actions in the Aggregate

01111001
01101111
01110101
01110010
01110111
01101111
01110010
01101100
01100100
01110100
01101111
01100011
01101000
01100001
01101110
01100111
01100101

Activism Transforms Digital: The Social Movement Perspective

Anastasia Kavada

Offering a flexible and decentralized communication infrastructure, the Internet seems to have a special affinity with the looser forms of organizing that characterize social movements. Facilitating rapid and cheap communication across geographical boundaries, the Internet can aid in transforming dissatisfaction to mass collective action quickly and efficiently. Online tools can help social movements find and disseminate information, recruit participants, organize, coordinate, and make decisions. However, this greater ease and speed of online communication does not necessarily lead to durable and stable activist networks, at least not in the traditional sense. Still, the regular organizing of face-to-face meetings, the maintenance of stable online spaces of memory and coordination, the cooperation around well-defined projects, as well as the creation of open narratives that describe the goals of the movement in ways that invite multiple interpretations help to make such networks more long-lasting.

Social Movements and Digital Activism

First, a brief note on terminology. Not only are social movements a difficult concept to define, but the term "social movement" is often used to describe a wide array of related phenomena, including protest events and coalitions. To add further complications, the field of social movement theory comprises diverse definitions of social movements—each associated with a different school of thought. However, as Mario Diani argues in his 1992 article "The Concept of Social Movement," all of these approaches agree that social movements:

- are made up by networks of informal interactions between diverse actors, including individuals, organizations, and groups;
- are bound by shared beliefs and ties of solidarity that make their participants attach a common meaning to specific collective events;
- are involved in political and/or cultural conflicts that arise as a result of social change.

Representing complex and enduring forms of collective action, social movements have a complicated relationship with digital technologies. They involve participants with disparate attitudes toward technology whose online practices evolve over time. They also employ online tools for a variety of purposes, including mobilization, coordination, and community building. Thus, focusing on social movements can provide a wider and more comprehensive view of the role of the Internet in collective action.

This role can be clearly seen in one of the major movements of the last decade: the Global Justice Movement (GJM), or antiglobalization movement as it is more widely, but inaccurately, known. The GJM is not opposed to globalization per se, but to the way it is shaped by the interests of large economic and political powers, which disregard the concerns of the poor and human rights and environmental issues. The movement has managed to connect diverse causes under its broad "Global Justice" umbrella. It involves activists from trade unions, autonomist groups, political parties of the radical left, and organizations concerned with human rights, environmentalism, poverty, and debt relief.

The GJM made its first well-publicized appearance in late 1999 during the "Battle of Seattle" where 50,000 demonstrators managed to severely disrupt the meeting of the World Trade

Organization. This was followed by demonstrations at almost every summit of a transnational economic organization or political power, including the International Monetary Fund, the World Bank, the Free Trade Area of the Americas, the EU, the G8, and the G20—the last two referring to meetings of the Group of the 8 or 20 most powerful economies in the world. Recent demonstrations include those organized around the London G20 summit in April 2009 and the G8 meeting held in Italy in July 2009. GJM activists also meet regularly in the social forums. These operate as an open platform where activists can network, share experiences, debate ideas, and formulate proposals for social change. The first World Social Forum was held in Brazil in 2001 and attracted thousands of participants. Its success inspired activists to set up regional and local social forums in other parts of the world, including Europe and the Americas.

Emerging in late 1999, at a time when Internet access was becoming more widespread, the GJM is considered to be one of the first movements to have organized extensively through the Internet. This has led observers to note that the way the GJM organizes has a special affinity with the modes of coordination facilitated by the Internet.

The Networked Structure of Social Movements

As "networks of informal interactions," social movements, such as GJM, tend to coordinate with a loose, flexible, and decentralized structure. Although the groups participating in them can have diverse organizational formats—from very hierarchical to very horizontal—when these groups coordinate with one another on the level of the movement, they tend to do so in a decentralized way. This was observed as early as in 1970, when Luther Gerlach and Virginia Hine, researchers from the University of Minnesota, suggested in *People, Power and Change* that the decentralized structure of social movements consists of the following characteristics:

- **Segmented**, meaning that social movements comprise numerous smaller groups (or, in the language of networks, "nodes") whose participation in the movement may wax and wane as new members join while others withdraw to focus on different interests.
- **Polycentric**, meaning that they have multiple centers and leaders whose influence tends to be temporary.
- **Integrated**, meaning that these multiple segments and hubs are connected to each other through interpersonal relationships between activists or through a common identity and a shared set of beliefs.

Called the SPIN model (an acronym referring to the main characteristics of decentralized structures (Segmented, Polycentric, INtegrated), the decentralized architecture described by Gerlach and Hine seems to apply to current social movements as well.

Decentralized structures seem to be facilitated and reinforced through the use of the Internet. In the case of the GJM, the Internet is thought to drive the movement toward more flexible and nonhierarchical types of organization, which reflect its own decentralized structure. For instance, according to Prof. Lance Bennett[1], the network that coordinated the Seattle protests was not a conventional organization but a "hyper-organization" that existed mainly online in the form of a tightly linked cluster of websites.

The drive toward more decentralized forms of organizing has been attributed both to the low cost of the Internet and its capacity for interactive and multimodal communication: Internet communication can range from synchronous to asynchronous, from mass to interpersonal, from local to global. Unlike other means of communication, the Internet cannot be centrally controlled. This facilitates the development of transnational, diverse, and loosely connected activist networks that are now able to organize protests and wage campaigns without a formal membership base, physical headquarters, or identifiable leaders.

The Capabilities of the Internet for Collectiv

The potential of the Internet for collective action re
range of social movement activities, including acces
seminating information, coordination and decision
well as building trust and a sense of collective identity.

ACCESSING AND DISCOVERING INFORMATION

Internet Capabilities for Discovering Information
- Increased access to publications, news stories, and reports
- More opportunities to discover information that is normally
  suppressed (e.g., through Wikileaks)
- Access to tools and platforms that help to monitor and share
  information (e.g., Google Alerts, Technorati, Digg, StumbleUpon,
  Del.icio.us)

Offering easy access to a variety of mainstream publications, news
stories, and reports, the Internet provides increased opportunities
for discovering relevant information. Furthermore, in their drive
to increase transparency, many government bodies have started
to make their official documents and public data available online.
The Internet also facilitates the discovery and leaking of information that is normally suppressed. Websites such as Wikileaks,
a version of Wikipedia that can distribute content across many
jurisdictions, allows whistle-blowers and journalists to release information about the unethical behavior of governments and corporations in a way that is impossible to trace and censor.

The Internet also provides a variety of tools that help to monitor, analyze, and visualize this information. For instance, Google
Alerts supplies email updates of the latest Google results about a
specific topic, helping activists to keep tabs on developing news
stories. Websites like Technorati can further be used to track popular content in the blogosphere and receive news from fellow activists, opponents, and the media. People can also share news, websites, and bookmarks through services like Digg, StumbleUpon

and Del.icio.us. All this allows activists to follow new developments, to find information about their opponents' wrongdoings, and to construct their case based on solid evidence.

DISSEMINATING INFORMATION AND REPORTING FROM THE STREETS

> **Five Key Practices for Disseminating Information**
> - Setting up a website for the campaign/cause/organization
> - Launching websites for specific events
> - Employing alternative media platforms (e.g., Indymedia)
> - Using blogging, micro-blogging, video, and photo-sharing platforms (e.g., Twitter, Blogger, YouTube, Flickr)
> - Making information "go viral" through email and social networking sites (e.g., MySpace, Facebook)

Apart from discovering and accessing information, the Internet also helps activists to disseminate their own content and to draw attention to their cause. The low cost of setting up a website allows social movements to more easily bypass the mainstream media by establishing their own news platforms. A pioneer of citizen journalism, Indymedia, is a well-known example. Based on the principles of open publishing, Indymedia enables activists to upload their own news stories and eyewitness reports. The platform was founded during the Battle of Seattle by a group of media activists who, dissatisfied with the coverage of the protest in the mainstream media, decided to set up their own website. The site was very successful, receiving two million hits during the Seattle protests. Since then, Indymedia has grown into a global network with more than one hundred fifty locally controlled news outlets.[2] Still, websites like Indymedia have a much lower number of pageviews than do mainstream news websites. Thus, in terms of reaching a wider public, the Internet does not necessarily free social movements from their reliance on the mainstream media.

Activists can also disseminate information about a specific protest by launching a website geared specifically to the needs of the event. Facilitated by the low cost of the medium, this is a very common practice within social movement organizing. Take, for instance, the protests around the 2009 G20 summit in London. These were coordinated by a loose coalition of forces that operated in partnership but organized parallel events. The coalition created a cluster of websites—Put People First, Meltdown in the City, Climate Camp, etc.—each one supportive of a specific event but providing links to the others. The websites offered a variety of information to prospective participants, including advice on what to carry on the day, downloadable maps of the protest sites, as well as cards outlining the protesters' legal rights in case of an arrest.

The emergence of blogging tools and micro-blogging platforms like Twitter have further expanded the potential of the Internet for circulating information. For example, during the 2009 G20 demonstrations in London, a collection of groups including Global Voices, Oxfam, and Blue State Digital recruited 50 bloggers from around the world to report from within the G20 summit. Called G20Voice, this initiative provided the public with a critical inside view of the summit discussions. Activists also used Twitter to disseminate the latest news about the protests, to convey their impressions from the street, and to send messages of solidarity. The broad coalition of nongovernmental organizations and voluntary groups that coordinated the Put People First demonstration, one of the many events organized around the G20 summit, published tweets in their websites providing live and up-to-the minute coverage of the event. In addition, video and photo-sharing sites, such as YouTube and Flickr, helped activists to upload visual material both before and after the protest. Transcending linguistic barriers and eliciting strong emotional reactions, the role of videos and photos is crucial for mobilization and for building a sense of collective identity.

Furthermore, the use of email and social networking sites such as Facebook and MySpace makes it easier for protest information to go viral. Activists can email mobilization messages to members of their social networks, asking them to forward the information to as many people as possible. Supporters can also publish such messages on their profiles in social networking sites and register their intention to participate in protests. The capacity for information to spread within existing social networks is crucial for mobilization because people are more prone to read messages from those that they know and trust. They are also more likely to participate in a protest when they know that their friends will also attend.

Apart from activating existing social networks, the Internet also facilitates the establishment of new ones. Email lists and Facebook groups help to create inclusive communication networks that allow anyone interested in the movement to be informed about its activities and to come in contact with other participants.

Blogs, social networking, and content-sharing sites decentralize the process of creating and disseminating information. They allow any activist with a laptop and a mobile phone to spread the word about the movement without having to go through more formal organizational channels. In his 2008 article for OpenDemocracy.net titled "The Alternative's Alternative," Evgeny Morozov, a leading thinker and commentator on the political implications of the Internet, noted that such tools can overshadow more centralized platforms like Indymedia and force them to play a different role in this complex information ecology. His suggestion was that rather than producing news, Indymedia should focus on aggregating and curating the thousands of blog posts, YouTube videos, and tweets circulating on the Net.

ACTIVISM BOTH ONLINE AND IN THE STREETS

In addition to mobilizing participation in street action, the Internet itself can become a site of action and civil disobedience. In his

2006 book *Internet Politics*, Andrew Chadwick, professor of political science at Royal Holloway, University of London, provides a roundup of such tactics. These include, among others, distributed-denial-of-service (DDoS) attacks or virtual sit-ins (flooding a website with too many simultaneous requests for data), and email bombing (paralyzing an organization's email system by bombarding its inbox with too many emails). In fact, it is not uncommon for activists to synchronize actions in the online realm with protest in the physical one. For example, during the Battle of Seattle, the Electrohippies Collective organized a DDoS attack on the computer network used by delegates to the World Trade Organization meeting. However, compared with street protests and demonstrations, tactics of "hacktivism" remain marginal within the Global Justice Movement.

COORDINATING AND MAKING DECISIONS

Internet Capabilities for Coordinating and Decision Making
- Allowing people to become members (by subscribing to an email list, joining a Facebook group, etc.)
- Offering a space for discussion on courses of action (on email lists, Facebook groups, Skype, etc.)
- Facilitating the scheduling of meetings and events (on email lists, through calendar-matching services, etc.)
- Enabling voting (through e-voting tools)
- Allowing the authoring and exchange of to-do lists

The Internet further helps activists to organize and make decisions. It facilitates processes of affiliation, allowing people to become members of the movement simply by subscribing to an email list or joining a Facebook group. Social movements have traditionally operated with an informal definition of membership. The ease with which activists can now join a protest network renders the process of affiliation even more fluid and flexible.

Online tools also aid collaboration, coordination, and the division of responsibilities among activists organizing a protest or campaign. Activists can use Wikipages to write to-do lists and messages of mobilization collaboratively. They can also employ calendar-matching services to plan meetings and gatherings. Interactive applications such as email, discussion groups, and instant messaging (and increasingly Internet telephony like Skype) can be used for decision making. Such collaboration can also be carried out through e-voting tools and other applications designed for aggregating preferences.

To meet their needs of coordination, social movements have also started to create their own Web platforms instead of using already existing ones that can only partly fulfill their needs. The European Social Forum launched such a platform in November 2007. Called OpenESF (www.openesf.net), the platform facilitates networking around common campaigns and initiatives by inviting registered users to create a profile and set up a project. These can refer to the preparation of the European Social Forum or to any proposal for social transformation as long as it conforms to the Charter of Principles of the World Social Forum. Projects are provided with a set of coordination tools including blogs, discussion lists, Wikipages, and task lists. As of August 2009, OpenESF had 970 registered members and 199 projects.

Spanning geographic boundaries, the Internet plays a vital role in coordinating protests across national borders. Still, activists often combine online tools with physical meetings, particularly for decisions that require lengthy discussion or negotiation among numerous participants. For instance, while Indymedia activists organize on the international level through email lists, instant messaging, and the Indymedia Twiki, local Indymedia groups also meet regularly face-to-face. The same mix of online and offline coordination is present in the European Social Forum, where activists employ both email lists and physical meetings in the process of decision making.

Movements organizing online face greater risks of surveillance and suppression. Tweets, Facebook groups, websites, and blogs are all available in the public domain. Thus, the same Internet tools that help social movements to keep track of their opponents' activities can also be used against them. For instance, during the 2009 G20 summit, the commander responsible for policing the protests admitted that the authorities were monitoring social networking sites. In an article published on BBC News Online, he said that such sites helped the police to assess the number of demonstrators expected in the streets and to get a sense of the activities being planned.[3]

BUILDING SOLIDARITY AND A SENSE OF COLLECTIVE IDENTITY

Facilitating interaction both on a group and on a one-to-one level, the Internet also helps activists to form and build interpersonal relationships and a sense of collective identity. Activists can circulate images, stories, and statements that convey the movement's mission, commemorate its landmark events, and name its allies and opponents. The Internet further allows activists to discuss and interact around these issues and to reflect on common experiences. Email lists, discussion groups, comments on Facebook and YouTube all contribute to this process of defining and identifying with the movement.

However, online discussions tend to be more prone to conflict than face-to-face contact. Interaction on email lists often involves the exchange of insults rather than opinions—a phenomenon called "flaming." Although a degree of conflict is necessary and expected in any social movement, flaming can disrupt group communication and dissolve relationships of trust.

The size of the online group and its degree of interpersonal communication also influence the kind of ties that can be created among its members. For instance, my analysis of three lists devoted to the organizing of the European Social Forum[4] has shown that it is easier for activists to share their opinions and feelings in smaller lists where they have a better sense of who is reading their messages. In contrast, the type of communication found in larger lists or Facebook wall comments is more suited to the development of abstract ties of solidarity. In their 2006 article for *Communication Monographs*, Andrew Flanagin, Cynthia Stohl, and Bruce Bimber, who have researched the role of technology in collective action organizations, call such ties "affiliative." These bonds arise when, in the absence of direct interpersonal relationships, activists still feel connected through their common affiliation with the movement.

THE IMPORTANCE OF ACTIVISTS' SKILLS, STRATEGIES, AND ATTITUDES

The way in which activists use online tools depends on their strategies and political culture. Particularly within such diverse movements as the GJM, participants may vary considerably in their attitudes toward the Internet. For instance, during the organizing of the European Social Forum in London in October 2004, British activists were divided into two camps whose opposing strategies were reflected in their use of online tools. Activists identifying themselves as Horizontals placed more emphasis on the process of organizing, noting that it should respect the values of openness, equality, and inclusiveness that characterizes the social forums. Their website expressed these ideals by incorporating more interactive features and by operating with a bottom-up process of content creation based on Wiki. The Verticals, on the other hand, were focused on creating a mass movement out of the European Social Forum. Their website was thus targeted to the wider public, aiming to offer authoritative information about the event. Its process of content creation was relatively top-down and monitored by the committee organizing the event to ensure the quality of information published on the site. So, we see that the capabilities of the Internet for social movement organizing are not inherent to the medium; they equally depend on the priorities, skills, and attitudes of the activists using it.

What Makes Online Movements Last?

Although indispensable for mobilization, the Internet often facilitates activist networks that are volatile, temporary, and unstable. The speed with which activists can spread information and organize action allows spontaneous mobilizations that draw large numbers but disappear as rapidly as they emerge. In his 2009 book *Communication Power*, Manuel Castells calls such networks "instant insurgent communities," noting the capacity of mobile and wireless communication to transform indignation into mass protest. Yet the loose and flexible structures formed online tend to dissolve after the protest ends. In addition, the fact that people can join a social movement with one click means that they can leave just as easily.

So, what can make such movements last? Within social movement theory, the standard answer to the question of durability is "more formal organization." Studies have shown that to endure through time, movements need to develop more rigid and bureaucratic organizational structures. However, for movements using the Internet extensively for organizing, the option of developing a more formal structure may not be a viable one. Thus, we are left with the following question: How can social movements establish stable and durable activist networks without losing their flexibility and informal character?

My sense is that to answer this question we need to perceive stability and continuity in more expansive terms. Movements last when the same people engaged in the same broad conflict are continuously working together, even if their specific protests shift in focus. But we can also say that movements survive when a constantly changing mix of activists is drawn under the same enduring slogan or cause. In other words, stability and continuity can be characteristics of the social networks that organize collective action or of the specific cause that brings them together. They can also refer to the time and space of organizing, including the rhythm of meeting up or the place where a movement gathers.

> **What Makes Online Movements Last?**
> - Open narratives and inclusive stories
> - Regular face-to-face meetings and events
> - Short-term and well-defined projects
> - A permanent online space

OPEN NARRATIVES AND INCLUSIVE STORIES

For movements organizing online, having a broad and open story in terms of their goals, mission, or seminal events allows them to maintain a steady flow of newcomers. Open narratives also invite multiple interpretations, making the movement attractive to a wide range of potential supporters. In their 2008 article, "Identity, Technology, and Narratives: Transnational Activism and Social Networks," Lance Bennett and Amoshaun Toft of the University of Washington note that open stories "enable both organizations and individuals to rely on social networking technologies to activate dense inter-organization and individual-level networks."[5] This increases the scale of the mobilization, helping to reenergize the movement as new activists join its ranks. The slogan of the social forums is a pertinent example here. Declaring that "Another World Is Possible," the social forums call on anyone who believes that there is an alternative to the injustices of the world to attend its meetings and events. Narratives can seem unconvincing, however, when they are not supported by the practices of the movement. Thus, the openness of the social forums is coupled with a mode of organizing that, at least in theory, emphasizes open and inclusive meetings, direct participation, and equality.

Open narratives further allow activist networks to shift their focus quickly and flexibly, thus making the most of new developments and opportunities. Email lists and Facebook groups created for a specific event construct a social network that can concentrate on a new target after the event has finished. The "Meltdown Facebook" group (short for Meltdown in the City—the London banking district), set up during the 2009 G20 summit by the more autonomous part of the alliance, is a good example. After the summit ended, the Facebook group, currently numbering more than thirty-five hundred members, was used to mobilize for other events, such as the Save Vestas Campaign—a mobilization in support of workers in the United Kingdom's only wind turbine blade factory after Vestas, the company that owns it, decided to close the plant.

REGULAR FACE-TO-FACE MEETINGS

The sheer number of websites, blogs, and email lists devoted to a social movement makes it almost impossible for individual activists to participate in every space. Accordingly, the movement becomes dispersed in the online realm. However, face-to-face meetings and street demonstrations can counterbalance such dispersion by bringing activists together in the same physical space at the same time. This strengthens feelings of belonging as it makes the collective a tangible reality, something that's more difficult to achieve online.

In addition, the prospect of meeting offline—and the organizing issues that need to be resolved before that can happen—as well as the need to report and reflect on events held face-to-face lead to an increase in online communication before and after offline gatherings. Therefore, when activists come together offline, they also converge online.

The regularity of offline meetings further strengthens the stability of a movement. The habit of meeting up at predictable intervals establishes a common rhythm of converging offline and dispersing online. For instance, the activists organizing the European Social Forum meet regularly face-to-face in the European Preparatory Assemblies held every three or four months in a different city around Europe. Thus, although the venue of the assembly or the mix of activists attending may change, the rhythm of meeting up renders the process more stable and predictable.

Physical meetings also accelerate the development of interpersonal relationships among activists. Face-to-face contact is rich in nonverbal cues that aid people in interpreting what others mean and assessing whether they're being truthful. In my interviews with activists of the European Social Forum, many of them emphasized the importance of "looking each other in the eyes" for trusting the words of others. Face-to-face contact also helps to resolve the conflicts arising online and repair the damage caused by flaming. It further facilitates agreement and consensus, leading to speedier negotiations among multiple parties. This is particularly important for decision making and explains why, despite the existence of sophisticated online tools, activists still feel the need to meet.

Furthermore, even within the same movement, activists maintain frequent contact with only a limited number of others, often those who they already know and trust or those who share their specific interests, nationality, age, or activist experience. While the Internet allows activists to disperse, following only the groups that they are most intimately involved in, face-to-face meetings force activists to communicate with a greater range of others. This helps the different segments of the movement to become more integrated and to endure through time.

SHORT-TERM AND WELL-DEFINED PROJECTS

Moreover, cooperation on short-term and well-defined projects helps activists to develop good working relationships. By focusing on a practical objective, movement participants are compelled to overcome their differences and to build trust based on the quality of their collaboration. The organizing of the European Social Forum offers such an objective to GJM activists. Held every one to two years in different European countries, the European Social Forum is predominantly organized by activists of the host country. This energizes the base of the movement in that country, bringing new participants to the European Social Forum process. Once the project finishes, the trust developed through these working relationships remains. This creates tighter activist networks that can stand the test of time by continuously focusing on new practical objectives. Even in cases where the group disperses once it fulfills its objective, the interpersonal links created through the project can be easily reactivated when a new protest opportunity arises.

A PERMANENT ONLINE SPACE

Finally, for movements lacking physical headquarters, having a permanent space online strengthens the sense of stability and continuity. Facebook groups, websites, and email lists serve as spaces of perpetual contact among activists located in different countries. They also help to ground and demarcate these fluid and flexible activist networks and act as gateways to the movement for both existing and new participants.

These online spaces also serve as sites of memory. They provide the movement with a sense of continuity by recording and archiving its discussions, statements, and activities. Websites created for specific events often remain long after the event is over. Frozen in time, these websites are transformed from live spaces of coordination to historical artifacts. This is a common practice within the European Social Forum process, whose main website (www.fse-esf.org) offers links to the websites of all the European Social Forum events organized so far.

Conclusion

Social movements are complex, loose, and fluid actors made up of networks of informal interactions among diverse participants. While online tools help them to organize in a decentralized way, they do not guarantee stability and continuity. Instead, they favor inclusive activist networks that evolve organically and easily shift their focus according to emerging opportunities.

The Internet can practically support such networks with its capacity for information-seeking and dissemination, for mobilization, coordination, and the building of a common identity. However, these capabilities are not inherent to online tools but depend on the skills, attitudes, and culture of the activists employing them. Despite the absence of a formal and institutionalized structure, social movements can still engage in certain practices that allow them to endure through time. Regular face-to-face gatherings, collaboration around short-term practical objectives, open narratives, and the maintenance of a permanent space online provide activist networks with more stability and continuity.

The Internet provides a communication infrastructure that can turn widespread dissatisfaction into a social movement. Even in movements organizing predominantly online, activists interact through a wide range of media and modes of communication. The ways in which social movements balance and coordinate their presence in these various communication spaces is central to their success and survival.

Notes

1. Lance Bennett, "Social Movements Beyond Borders: Understanding Two Eras of Transnational Activism" in *Transnational Protest and Global Activism*, ed. D. della Porta and S. Tarrow, 203–226 (New York and Oxford: Rowman & Littlefield, 2005).

2. However, it is worth noting that according to its central website, www. Indymedia.org, Indymedia is not "a conscious mouthpiece of any particular point of view," even though "many Indymedia organizers and people who post to the Indymedia newswires are supporters of the 'anti-globalization' (alternative globalization, anti-corporatization) movement."

3. L. Rodgers, "Eco-Activists Prepare for Protest." (BBC News Online, March 27, 2009). Available at http://news.bbc.co.uk/1/hi/uk/7961868.stm (Accessed August 15, 2009).

4. For more information, see Anastasia Kavada, "Email Lists and the Construction of an Open and Multifaceted Identity: The Case of the London 2004 European Social Forum," *Information, Communication & Society* 12, no. 6 (2009): 817–839.

5. Lance Bennett and Amoshaun Toft, "Identity, Technology, and Narratives: Transnational Activism and Social Networks," in *Handbook of Internet Politics*, A. Chadwick and P. N. Howard (London and New York: Routledge, 2008): 246–260.

Digital Transforms Activism: The Web Ecology Perspective

Tim Hwang

Based in New Hampshire, The Mountain is a small American casual apparel company that produces a wide variety of wildlife-themed shirts. One of their shirts, Three Wolf Moon, is dark forest green with an elaborate design of three wolves, surrounded by stardust, howling at the Moon. This shirt and the company's other products were originally posted online for sale in a sleepy corner of Amazon.com. On November 10, 2008, one sarcastic viewer, giving the shirt an extraordinarily high rating, wrote:

> This item has wolves on it which makes it intrinsically sweet and worth 5 stars by itself, but once I tried it on, that's when the magic happened. After checking to ensure that the shirt would properly cover my girth, I walked from my trailer to Wal-mart [sic] with the shirt on and was immediately approached by women. The women knew from the wolves on my shirt that I, like a wolf, am a mysterious loner who knows how to "howl at the moon" from time to time (if you catch my drift!). The women that approached me wanted to know if I would be their boyfriend and/or give them money for something they called mehth [sic]. I told them no, because they didn't have enough teeth, and frankly a man with a wolf-shirt shouldn't settle for the first thing that comes to him.

This write-up would, by itself, be of no particular note: the Internet is brimming with this kind of gently (or not-so-gently) mocking activity. What was surprising, however, was the extent to which this single review was only one of the early strikes in an enormous wave of reviews that would come crashing down on the product page over the next few months.

Driven by a few key online communities and massive distribution over Twitter, reviewing the shirt exploded as an extraordinarily popular online activity. Before it was all over, the product had logged more than one thousand reviews, all ironically claiming everything from miraculous healing powers to increased sexual prowess gained by wearing the Three Wolf Moon shirt.

Even more startling than the sheer number of reviews was the impact of this cultural craze on sales. The company saw a massive spike in orders, pushing the shirt past such perennial hits as the Crocs brand rubber sandal to become the top product on the Amazon Apparel Bestsellers list for more than three weeks. The practice of leaving ridiculously over-the-top reviews also spread outward to other products The Mountain offered. One shirt, the Breakthrough Wolf model, featured an image of a lone gray wolf that appeared to burst forth from the wearer's chest. "DO NOT BUY THIS SHIRT," one reviewer complained, "It is a rip-off. For the same price you can have three wolves on it." The reviewer left a one star rating.

Many ambiguities continue to surround this cultural explosion and how it came to be, but what's obvious was that The Mountain was taken completely and utterly by surprise. The company had not planned for this nor was it quite sure what to make of it all as sales of the previously unpopular shirt soared.

From the point of view of the scholar or practitioner of digital activism, the Three Wolf Moon case, and the many stories similar to it that have appeared in popular Internet culture during the past few years, are as exciting as they are disconcerting.

On one hand, clearly these types of cultural "explosions" are tapping into a vast pool of effort, creativity, energy, and motivation latent in online spaces and communities. Moreover, events like the Three Wolf Moon shirt require more than just a trivial amount of time and effort. In this and many other cases, individuals are willing to devote significant material resources to a particular activity, as well as to expend a considerable amount of creativity and attention to following an evolving social phenomenon. What's exciting for activists is that they, too, might be able to find some way to harness and direct even a tiny piece of the energy that manifests itself in the bustle of popular Internet culture.

An element of unpredictability is present, however, that is fairly unsettling to an activist or a researcher in political mobilization. Many of the groups that seem to form around popular Internet culture are nearly instantaneous, seemingly without leaders, and appear without any particular rhyme or reason. Needless to say, these phenomena are surprising from a traditional view of leadership and the slow, deliberate methods we usually associate with the mobilization of individuals around a cause. How might we consciously replicate this kind of cultural activity? Few analytical tools are available to approach this space, and we are, accordingly, often prevented from taking a more rigorous approach to understanding how and why events online evolve as they do.

The obvious human energy that powers the vibrant social ecosystem of the Web, the phenomena appearing within it, and the popular culture of the Internet are worth studying more closely in their broad outlines and in specific instances. I want to go one step beyond just considering Web culture as an interesting topic of exploration. Specifically, I want to argue that where digital activism is concerned, an understanding of Web culture is absolutely key to effectively operating online. This might seem like a gross exaggeration—after all, what does an amusing anecdote about a silly shirt really have to do with the serious work of campaigning for political office or organizing against a repressive regime?

To answer that question, we must take a step back. If activism is the activation of groups of individuals to achieve a collective aim, then activism in a fundamental sense relies on engaging the underlying forces of community and culture at work in a particular media or space. An activist trying to get the word out about a particular issue in traditional media, for example, will be best equipped when armed with the knowledge of how communities and cultures form around television broadcasts and how best to present information within that medium.

So, considering online space to be another kind of media, what is crucial is to master the forces of culture and community at work to effectively operate online. Ultimately, what is most telling about the case of the Three Wolf Moon shirt is realizing that it is not an isolated incident. Indeed, the kind of massive mobilization, provisional organization around an activity, and rapid speed of action are characteristic of a pattern of online cultural behavior that experts have dubbed "viral"—likening such phenomena to the sudden, exponential spread of viruses in a biological ecosystem. The explosive viral growth of content and, indeed, the dynamics of more sustained, "merely" social communities online encapsulate in some sense the very mechanisms that activists of all types hope to mobilize. Whether a dedicated group emerges around an amusing T-shirt or a presidential candidate doesn't matter, since our interest is in the deeper-rooted mechanisms of how groups form and culture flows through an online social system. That some of the most dramatic mobilizations on the Web have accumulated around humorous pictures of cats or long-lost '80s pop stars should hint at a deeper lesson that activists can learn.

From this initial premise, this chapter draws on the work of the Web Ecology Project, an emerging research group that is beginning to approach the challenge of gaining a better understanding of cyberspace precisely by embracing a serious study of the underlying online social forces that are at the root of both cultural fads and more serious activism against established authorities.

Based in Boston, the Web Ecology Project was founded in late 2008 as an effort to establish and foster an international community of practitioners and researchers that could support this type of research, as well as work in the interest of actually creating practical tools and methods that could be deployed for shaping the flows of culture and community online. Initially, the group worked to take stock of the huge body of research and debate that had accumulated about culture and communities online in the past decade and determine where a dedicated group of researchers could be useful to other scholars working in the space. The first questions addressed were: What weaknesses are present in the current research about the Web? How might we create an approach to potentially improve such research?

This chapter is designed to be a crash course on how this emerging research into social networks and culture online might provide serious insight into the methods of online activism. First, we will review some of the research and explore its immediate practical applications to activism in terms of organization and practice. Second, we will discuss how some of this quantitative research about the structure of online culture and content suggests the potential creation of an entirely new generation of tools for online activism. Finally, we will conclude by discussing some of the ethical considerations that come with pursuing these new tools and methods—and also look at some suggestions for mitigating them. We will also address some of the potential weaknesses in the Web ecological approach and investigate areas that invite more extensive study.

Initial Lessons from the Web Ecology Project

So far we've talked in rather abstract terms about the connection between Web culture and digital activism. Now we turn to making the link between the two more concrete to better illustrate how research on the former might have significant practical applications for the day-to-day strategy and tactics of the latter. Drawing on some of the latest work of the Web Ecology Project, this section distills two big lessons about mobilizing people online that have emerged from our research. The studies I'm using all examine the different aspects of conversations on Twitter—both because these reports have interesting broader implications for working with community and culture online and in the interest of minimizing the amount of jargon that would pop up in jumping from platform to platform in the discussion.

MEMETIC ENTROPY: THE CHALLENGE OF TOO MUCH PARTICIPATION

One immediate question that comes to mind is whether or not research can inform our mental checklist of relevant concerns when we're launching a campaign online. How do we foster conversation online? What do we do once we've begun dialogues?

For one of the Web Ecology Project's first reports, we conducted an overview of the Twitter conversation happening around Iran's recent postelection crisis. Working with a set of more than two million tweets (short posts) produced by users, our study captured the universe of content created in the weeks leading up to and directly after the election. Rather than focus tightly on content produced by activists in Iran and around the world, our group attempted to enlarge the scope of the study by examining the broader cultural landscape of discussion around the topic. This included the activists, certainly, but also incorporated the commentary of celebrities, journalists, casual observers, and many others. This examination revealed that the biggest issue facing some activists was not so much getting the word out—where an issue strikes a nerve with a large enough audience, content spreads easily. Instead, the threat came from the door to participating in the conversation being open to contributions from all sides, whether or not they are constructive or useful. Indeed, in an era of social platforms that are tightly networked, the bar to merely getting a message out from a circle of activists into the public sphere is much lower. Consequently, on increasingly popular platforms like Twitter, the period between when a conversation becomes widespread or trending and the point at which it becomes "polluted" with a high amount of noise in the form of spam and tangential conversation is rapidly shrinking.

This problem is particularly significant to the work of activists, since any goal beyond "fostering discussion" online will require that certain kinds of information be far more important to spread than others. Particularly where a campaign attempts to motivate people to real-world action, a massive, unfocused discussion around a topic might, in fact, hide or inhibit effective mobilization. This happened quickly in the case of the discussion around Iran—the initial voices of activists reporting on events from within the country became rapidly washed out in the noise of the commentary from a mostly U.S- and Europe-based group of reporters and celebrities (with some standout exceptions, including, most notably, @persiankiwi, an anonymous opposition Iranian activist reporting about events on the ground during the crisis). For the interested viewer, however, a casual glance at the stream of content emerging about the Iran election on Twitter would be overwhelming—impossible to keep up with and read, and most of it would not actually be from the activists on the ground.

This phenomenon is not confined to conversations about "serious" topics or political issues. A common occurrence on the Web is the flurry of reposting, commenting, and spam that springs up around a particular piece of popular content, which inhibits the ability of an interested reader to assess where, when, and why content is being created. Most important, without any particular intervention, the most relevant and actionable content often becomes increasingly obscured—a process that we call "memetic entropy." The word "entropy" refers to the process of disorganization, "memetic" comes from the word "meme," a transmittable unit of cultural content. Thus, memetic entropy refers to the observation that the dissemination of cultural content itself seems to engender an increasing disorganization of that very content, in this case because no limits on participation in dissemination are present, and, as a result, no way is available to clearly identify which user-generated content is most salient to the activist.

A simple but useful lesson for the online activist: build methods of filtration and curation into an overall strategy of awareness and mobilization. While a rapidly spreading discussion online might foster awareness, creating easy access to relevant information and ways to sift through information in a semi-stable way play a key role in sustaining attention. After all, the question isn't just whether or not a group of activists can get the word out, but whether or not those activists get the proper information to the right people once the spotlight of attention is turned on them.

VARIETIES OF ONLINE INFLUENCE

A now-standard method of spreading an idea online is a kind of "shotgun strategy"—in which a group of users fan out, attempting to send a given email or piece of content to everyone they are linked to in the social space of the Web in a short time. The general concept is that a sufficiently large wave of shared content will translate into a cascade of action. This anticipated outcome implicitly assumes that a big enough readership necessarily translates into social influence.

However, particularly online, only a weak correlation exists between the two, and the dimensions of influence are far more varied. Some online communities, in terms of absolute number of members, are nearly insignificant to the broad landscape of the Web but they are able to motivate their users to expend intense effort on achieving a given goal. In contrast, the online presences of some prominent individuals still act mostly as broadcast media—behaving in a noninteractive pattern that we usually associate with older, more mainstream media outlets.

This argument isn't to assert that one kind of influence is more or less important than another. Instead, the different types of influence online should be viewed as tools that are advantageous for initiating certain kinds of action. To that end, activists should tailor how they spread information depending on the kinds of social outcomes they want to achieve. Is the campaign one to simply raise awareness? Or will it only be successful with the participation of the audience?

Let's take a closer look at the varieties of influence at work in the online ecosystem. A recent Web Ecology Project experiment, The Influentials, took a close look at the interaction between users commonly accepted to be "the most important" on Twitter and their audience. Specifically, the report determined how a given tweet sent by one of these users generated different mixtures and patterns of activity in the online social space.

Monitoring the behavior of these influential users and their audience over 10 days, we divided user reactions to the content produced by "influentials" into three categories. The "re-tweet," which was marked when users merely repeated content posted by these top individuals or organizations. The "reply," which was charted when users responded to a given piece of content with a comment or question directed at these influencers. And, finally, the "mention," which captured where users referenced the "influentials" without necessarily directing anything toward them. We also tracked when content was sent by these "influentials" over the 10 days. Combining this data allowed us to visualize the distinct bursts of social activity that quickly follow the release of content by one of these users.

Working with even a small set of extremely popular Twitter "celebrities" and monitoring them for a relatively short time revealed a remarkable diversity of social activity. This despite the fact that these users are often lumped together in the popular press as an undifferentiated group of top Twitter users noted for their large numbers of followers. Furthermore, the user responses to these celebrities form distinct patterns. Some, like the wildly popular technology industry blog "Mashable" and the prominent social media consultant Chris Brogan, seem to consistently generate social activity in response to their content across the entire spectrum. In particular, their audiences respond to their content with a balanced mixture of re-tweets, replies, and mentions in a pattern of short, concentrated bursts. In contrast, users like the prominent technology commentator iJustine and noted wine entrepreneur Gary Vee see a more consistent, sustained level of social activity around their content in terms of replies and mentions. However, they do not experience the repetition and spreading of their content that other top users do. We could have mapped many other dimensions, but one clear takeaway is that "influence" is far from homogenous online. Indeed, the specific blend of the content users spread and the audience that surrounds them is a critical part of how various types of engagement evolve online.

What applies to individuals or news outlets also applies to the use of platforms. Particularly in the world of technology, the media darling of the moment sometimes seems like the "cure-all" tool for gathering a community. While no doubt deploying a Wiki, blog, Twitter account, Facebook presence, or Second Life island might significantly bolster coordination and promote action, it's important to recognize that these are specific tools that come with their own advantages and limitations that emerge from how they structure communication. One stark reminder of this was an examination of the tweets surrounding the death of Michael Jackson. When a group of individuals was asked to assess whether or not tweets expressed sadness, respondents could not consistently agree on the emotion expressed in approximately 32 percent of the tweets. Such ambiguity seems to arise because Twitter constrains communication between users to 140 character blocks. Certain modes of expression appear more amenable to being expressed in such limited space. This seems to apply both to the content of what is being expressed and to the grammatical structure of the content. We found, for example, that tweets that referenced multiple events in connection to Michael Jackson created more disagreement between readers than ones that focused solely on his death. Taking a wider scope, the study suggests that social platforms in general vary in their relative ability to communicate certain types of information. Although more research is required to pin down more definitively the details of these differences, an important parallel occurs in the realm of platforms, which may create distinct social results the same way that individual users do.

Regardless, the broader lesson here is that the social outcomes generated by the release of content depend critically on the audience and the structure of the platform that acts as the clearinghouse for the information. Particularly when a group's human resources and time might be extremely limited, an all-encompassing shotgun strategy of spreading the word to every contact and across every social service might be a relatively high cost and low benefit course of action. Moreover, the risk that a campaign of broadly contacting as many people as possible might actually backfire is always present. Activists who indiscriminately and frequently send out content might see diminishing returns as recipients lose interest and become more likely to disregard information.

Being targeted about the aims of the campaign, then, and analyzing communities and platforms in this more deliberate way might offer better chances for communicating through online space. As knowledge about such communications expands, so will the ability to be more discriminating and effective in spreading a message or advocating for action online. Interestingly, some emerging work suggests that such quantitative data on the type of influence a given user can exert might be generated quickly for any given target and in a way that regularly updates with new information emerging online. This hints at an entirely new generation of "activist technologies"—tools that might aid activists in navigating the complexities of the online social space and make better decisions about how to interact with and use it.

New Activist Technologies

A PRESCRIPTION FOR "GOING VIRAL"?

This quantitative, data-driven approach has applications beyond merely suggesting some useful though informal rules for how activists should approach campaigning online. It also opens the door to creating a novel set of tools for activists looking to both navigate and mobilize communities in online spaces more effectively. This section will discuss some of the most promising efforts currently being pursued and some of the future "activist technologies" that look increasingly possible as research goes forward.

The first is a series of tools that might aid activists in producing and promoting material that is more likely to achieve the kind of wild popularity evident in the Three Wolf Moon case. Three Wolf Moon has been a topic of intense scrutiny in the past, particularly in the marketing and advertising industry, though much of the work in creating "viral" videos remains an imperfect art at best. A more quantitative, data-driven approach might be more helpful. By observing trends as they emerge and capturing data on how and what types of users participate in the spreading of content across a broad landscape of examples, generating a typology of how pieces of content and certain practices quickly gain massive following becomes possible. Some of the work that examined Twitter during Iran's postelection crisis discussed above demonstrates this. By monitoring the conversations happening online and identifying the most referenced users in the discussion, researchers were able to derive some basic statistics about the rise of various users to positions of prominence as well as the structure of the overall discussion. Once a template is fashioned, data must be consistently gathered on topics as they become popular—this will enable researchers to get a larger sense of what drives these kind of phenomena. Such data include not just highly publicized instances of political turmoil like the Iran case, but also the ephemera of jokes and odd news stories that are passed around daily. What is also possible is to use this strategy with other platforms, e.g., YouTube, to observe how many videos with unusually fast growth in viewership behave and how rapidly they are passed around. This landscape study will allow us to understand whether the cultural phenomena that become wildly popular operate in a distinct way in different platforms or are just the most prominent patterns of a whole spectrum of more or less viral content.

This description might conjure up ambitious visions of a foolproof method that can reliably create consistently popular online hits every time. Currently, too many variables are present, so creating a model for "bottling" viral growth is not feasible. However, we must recognize that some of the numbers most useful to an activist are actually relatively low-hanging fruit from a research point of view. Even some rough simple data on how much activity is happening at a given time on a social network may help individuals know when to best release their material to get the best pickup among users. In the same way that politicians and their staffs are aware of the nature of and employ the news cycle in promoting a story to a headline or relegating it to a back page, so, too, might large-scale data mining reveal similar patterns in online spaces that might be useful to activists. A scan of social media activity on Twitter during the postelection turmoil in Iran, for instance, identified two repeated peaks that occurred throughout the day and signaled the possibility of a promising time to reach a community interested in that particular topic.[1] An application could be designed for any social platform to assist activists in processing large amounts of past data and automatically recommending the high activity times for particular topics and issues as good opportunities to take advantage of the Web's news cycle.

MAPPING THE CONVERSATIONAL LANDSCAPE

Another useful piece of activist technology that might emerge from the analysis of online social dynamics is the potential to build an application that dynamically visualizes the conversation around particular issues across various social platforms on the web. Such an application, for instance, might allow an activist to see, at a glance, who online was currently supporting either side of the debate over public health care, and who was most influential in that discussion across blogs, Twitter, or even the comments of a given website. On the campaign level, these types of tools might form the basis for a kind of activist "political terrain map" that could generate a sense of the relative standing of activists within a community and identify who on a given platform might be natural allies to engage and partner with. Such software would also allow the quick identification of the influential players in an online social ecosystem and potentially unearth some hidden influencers who might not be immediately obvious (or might be receiving less press attention).

HACKING INFLUENCE

Latent opportunities exist in "hacking" the markers of influence or prominence in certain social systems. The number of followers on Twitter, for example, and the comparison of that value against the number of users a given account is following, is often used as an informal measure for authenticity and influence. However, the widespread practice of using "autofollowing"—a basic script that automatically tracks any user who follows a given account—creates a vulnerability to this value system. A simple program can be deployed to search Twitter and generate a regularly updated index of all the accounts across the service that autofollow. A new user can activate all these accounts at once, instantaneously creating the appearance of a massively credible, massively authoritative account.

These ways of short-circuiting the indicators for influence are powerful tools for a small group of activists, particularly when they are moving to challenge an established authority that is less familiar with the online social media space. More sophisticated versions of these methods, which could leverage networks of seemingly "influential" accounts, might make it more difficult for an authority to react effectively while concurrently serving to mask the true identities of various actors.

A SOCIAL "RADAR" FOR ONLINE ACTIVISTS?

None of the tools described above will allow activists to do anything truly novel: effective activists have always attempted to identify ideal times to release information, track influential players, and utilize free opportunities to spread their message in a space. A succinct description of the above projects: They are working to bolster the existing efforts at community management and organizing with data-driven methods and applications. Nonetheless, having these types of tools available remains important because it provides an opportunity to take better advantage of the powerful emergent qualities of the Web's social environment. While a basic level of new media literacy no doubt provides the skills and best practices to develop a blog or effectively coordinate groups of people via SMS, these new activist technologies provide the vital information about how to effectively deploy these skills in a given situation. These technologies may provide activists with a vastly expanded sense of how their activity fits into a much broader social framework of culture and community on the Web. They add a "radar" to the online activist's toolkit—an aid to visualizing, examining, and strategizing about the best way to navigate the Internet's otherwise opaque social landscape. This kind of analysis is also particularly feasible in the online space, where users generate huge quantities of accessible data about their social behavior.

Such attempt to turn community management and engagement into a kind of quantifiable science also holds another exciting possibility: reproducibility as a way of proving claims. Reproducibility is a particularly interesting concept in this context. It implies knowledge of a certain method, A, that will reliably create a given social phenomenon, B. The current state of research is still far from reliably producing a planned-for effect. Yet, an example of some future prospects is worth examining to give an idea of where some of the research described might lead and how it might support the work of activists.

Where the methods to reproduce social phenomena might be mechanized and scriptable, the possibility of creating "social engines"—scripts that automatically foster community or promote certain types of collective behavior—arises. Realboy is one early example of what such a system might look like. The project is an experimental piece of software that can take control of a Twitter account and make it perform an automated, robotic series of actions, creating a presence on Twitter that is believable to users. Employing a simple system of social network analysis to generate content, Realboy can reliably gather in an audience of users that "follow" it online. A more sophisticated future iteration might be able to aggregate online communities by speaking consistently about certain issues and displaying some basic believable behaviors that would invite responses and participation from an online following. A goal would be to allow a user to activate these scripts online, step away, and return a few months later to find an active, connected community ready to be mobilized to achieve a stated aim.

As discussed at the beginning of the chapter, Web Ecology and the research being done in a variety of fields attempt to focus on the underlying dynamics at work in online social behavior. No particular deterministic quality inheres to the tools arising from research that requires them to be used either for constructive or descriptive purposes. Indeed, the concept of effective "community engines" fostering and harvesting groups of individuals automatically raises some important ethical considerations.

Ethical Considerations and Conclusion

The new generation of activist tools outlined here is both a blessing and a curse in a very real sense. The same tools that empower small groups of citizens to shape and influence large-scale social systems online are the very same that could be used by established authorities to confound attempts to remove those same officials. These technologies also have a commercial viability to them that raises some question about their use in exploiting personal information for financial gain. The large-scale data mining that creates the ability to know when people are more likely to pick up content or to identify the strong influencers in a given network can, for example, be used to advocate for social reform or by a company looking to promote its next product.

One concern of this work is that the private development of these tools or the publication of research in a way that is difficult for a nontechnical reader to understand might result in more harm than good. Awareness of these methods and access to easy-to-use tools is one way of addressing some of the ethical concerns that plague the applications of this work. For that purpose, as Web Ecology has moved forward, one of its strategies has been to make an ethical commitment to open publication, sharing of data, and the creation of easy to access, user friendly metrics and tools.

Another unspoken caveat is worth making explicit: while no doubt the development of these new tools holds great prospects and great dangers, it's worthwhile to point out that the Web isn't everything, particularly where online activism is concerned. The ability to effect real change relies partly on the ability of organizers to effectively communicate and engage communities but also depends crucially on being able to motivate people to take action in the real world. Accordingly, the current work of Web Ecology, in its focus on system-wide flows of culture and the formation of communities online, does leave some important questions unanswered about how motivation manifests as action in the real world. It also fails to address persistent centers of power that are mostly offline and their relative ability to repress or radically change the terms of the online and offline environment that activists work in.

That being said, the work described here is just an initial foray; future research will likely (if not necessarily) have to account for the larger motivations that translate to real-world action and the power structures that exist therein. Ultimately, the Web is a data-rich environment that gives us an initial handle on the previously difficult-to-measure mechanisms of group behavior. Indeed, the identification of those principles in Web space may be the first step in understanding how they function in the real world as well.

Notes

1. The Web Ecology Project, "The Iran Election on Twitter: The First Eighteen Days," http://www.webecologyproject.org/2009/06/iran-election-on-twitter/ (accessed Aug 15, 2009).

Destructive Activism: The Double-Edged Sword of Digital Tactics

Steven Murdoch

On April 27, 2007, a group of websites in Estonia, including those of media outlets, government ministries, and banks, went offline. For three weeks, these sites were the target of a highly effective attack triggered by the government's controversial decision to move a Soviet war memorial. Similar attacks were experienced in August 2008, targeting Georgian websites during that country's conflict with Russia over the control of South Ossetia. In both cases, the Russian government was initially blamed, but eventually it became clear that "patriotic hackers" (sometimes known has "hacktivists") were the likely culprits. While the impact of these cyber-attacks was significant, criminal attacks of even greater magnitude were commonplace on the Internet at the time and continue to be a problem. The attacks in Estonia and Georgia, however, distinguish themselves by being motivated by political activism rather than criminal intent.

So far this book has viewed the empowerment of citizens through digital means as largely positive. However, the ability of the Internet to share information, coordinate action, and launch transnational campaigns can also be used for destructive ends.

This chapter describes how some of the tactics adopted by digital activists have been used to disrupt communications, deface or destroy virtual property, organize malicious actions offline, and publish personal information or disinformation. Actions that cause physical harm to human beings or endanger property have yet to be engaged as a tactic of activism, but this chapter will describe how other groups have taken this route. We address physical harm in this chapter because its represents the next frontier of destructive digital activism.

We often view digital activism as a series of positive practices that have the power to remedy injustice. However, digital tools—and the very infrastructure of the Internet—are value neutral and can be used for a variety of activities. The tools and practices can thus be seen as a double-edged sword to be used constructively or destructively. This dual nature raises ethical questions that I will address at the end of the chapter.

Tactics

In this chapter, destructive digital activism is divided into five categories: blocking access; destroying and defacing virtual property; organizing malicious activity; misusing information; and attacking critical infrastructure. In each of these forms of destructive activism, the inherent capacities of the Internet are manipulated to cause harm either to persons or property. In the case of blocking access, particularly the distributed denial of service (DDoS) attack, the protocol by which information is requested from a website is misused to overwhelm the response capacity of the site's server and prevent the site from responding to legitimate requests—in effect, shutting down the site. In the case of destroying and defacing property, the server on which the website is stored is again the target of the attack, though in this case the server—which is little more than a specialized computer—is hacked in order to gain access to and vandalize the site's code.

In the case of organizing malicious activities, the infrastructure of the Internet is used to allow cooperation when more conventional means, such as meeting in person, are inconvenient or impossible. Anonymous discussion boards and encryption software help activists (who are acting in the public interest) in repressive countries to evade government surveillance; they may also be used to protect activist groups acting against the public interest, such as fascist political parties, from being regulated by the government. These technologies are, as stated earlier, value neutral and protect users regardless of motive or action.

In the opposite scenario, activists can forcibly "out" their adversaries by exposing and disseminating their personal information on the Internet. Here, the same network in which anonymous communication software operates so effectively is used to make available personal information and even misinformation. Anonymous communication software can be deployed because of the "end to end" architecture of the Internet. Within this structure, intelligence lies in the end devices, which can be rapidly upgraded with new functionality without waiting for the network to upgrade, too. This dramatically increases the speed at which new technologies can be developed, but also means that end devices are more complex and thus more vulnerable to attack. Not surprisingly, the intelligent devices at the edge of the network can be compromised by the introduction of malicious software or by hacking into the system from a remote location—two techniques for causing damage to critical infrastructure.

Just as the digital activists discussed in the rest of this book have co-opted the infrastructure of the Internet to fight injustice and defend human rights, the activists in this chapter use the same infrastructure to orchestrate attacks on individuals, institutions, and even countries. Often using software perfected by criminals, they bend the Internet to their own more sinister goals.

BLOCKING ACCESS

The primary technique used in the Estonian attacks was the distributed denial of service attack, one of the most common forms of destructive digital activism. In a DDoS attack, a large number of computers controlled by the attacker are commanded to overload a single computer with Internet traffic. Normally the computers used to execute the attack are not owned by the attacker but belong to innocent parties who have had their PC hacked into by malicious software (malware) carried by spam or downloaded unintentionally from a malicious website. This network of compromised computers, known as a "botnet," can be remotely directed to send out spam to enlarge the network, carry out DDoS attacks, or do anything else its creator wishes.

The Estonian DDoS attack was hailed as the first cyber-war, but, in fact, nation-states have been attacking the computing infrastructure of their opponents for decades using far more sophisticated techniques. What makes Estonia interesting is that the capability to carry out coordinated attacks on significant online targets was shown to be available to ordinary citizens.

DDoS attacks and botnets were first used by pranksters, in minor squabbles between geeks and as demonstrations of technical skills. Their impact on the general public was minimal. This changed when criminals moved in and decided to make money. They refined the tools, scaled them up, and made them easier to use. Criminals would attack a major website (online gambling sites were a popular target) and demand payment to stop the DDoS. This lucrative illicit business led to significant enhancements in malware technology. Once the tools and techniques were developed by criminals and became easier to use, they were adopted by activists, who chose political rather than financial targets.

Most applications used in digital activism are not created for activist purposes: Facebook groups to organize protests and smart phones to take video of police abuses are two examples of commercial software and hardware now employed for activist purposes. Software used for DDoS attacks also originated in a field outside of activism, though the purposes of development were criminal rather than commercial.

DDoS attacks also share similarities to offline protests. Rather than recruiting unwitting victims to the botnet, some activists openly solicit volunteers by stating their cause and asking for support. Those who consent can download software that will carry out the attacks on their behalf. Sometimes volunteers are simply asked to visit a particular website and click "refresh," thus overloading the website with page requests. While this type of attack doesn't cause the same levels of traffic as a bot attack, it is much harder to distinguish from legitimate usage, which, in turn, makes it harder to filter out malicious Internet traffic before it reaches the website.

DESTROYING AND DEFACING VIRTUAL PROPERTY

Other techniques activists have used to protest the actions of their target include website defacement, analogous to the vandalism that might accompany protests. Here, someone hacks into the server hosting the site and alters the content. For example, during the Georgian conflict, an activist group supporting Russia replaced the site of the Georgian Parliament with pictures of Adolf Hitler. The development of tools for hacking has followed the same pattern as that of DDoS attacks: first, these techniques were used on a small scale by geeks, then monetized by criminals, then adopted by activists. Criminal gangs would use hacked servers for hosting illicit information or to steal confidential data and sell it. Now, activists use the same tools and techniques developed by criminals for carrying out politically motivated actions.

While the Georgian and Estonian attacks were short-lived, others are part of prolonged conflict. For example, in the Israel-Palestine "Interfada" of 2000, hackers supporting both Israel and Palestine attacked the opposing government's websites. These attacks included not only spam and DDoS attacks, but also website defacement. Attacks have grown in sophistication since then and now incorporate characteristics of psychological warfare and propaganda.

ORGANIZING MALICIOUS ACTIVITY

Carrying out effective attacks of any type requires coordination. Here, the Internet also proves very useful because online forums and email offer an easy and inexpensive means to marshal forces. In addition, easily available encryption and anonymous communication software can resist surveillance, and, in practice, the sheer quantity of information flowing over the Internet is a major obstacle to effective surveillance for any but the most sophisticated intelligence services. This allows activists who are the target of surveillance, by either law enforcement or corporate security personnel, to organize while reducing the risk of their actions being disrupted; it also helps activists operating in repressive regimes but concurrently benefits criminals. Governments fear that criminals might use the Internet to evade legitimate surveillance just as activists use the Internet to evade illegitimate and politically motivated surveillance. The ability of criminals to evade conventional surveillance, like telephone taps, by communicating over the Internet has led to legislation in many countries. For example, in the United Kingdom, suspects can be forced to disclose encryption passwords. This law has been used to threaten animal rights activists found with encrypted data that the police believe might be of use in a criminal investigation if decrypted.

The Internet's usefulness in organizing with a lesser likelihood of surveillance benefits both activists and criminals. Terrorists also use websites to recruit followers and advertise training camps. In fact, the effectiveness of the Internet for the dissemination of information means that damage can be caused even without disrupting communications.

One group that uses the Internet to organize what some have construed as malicious activity calls itself "Anonymous." It has no central control; instead members self-identify and cluster around actions for which there is a critical mass of activists. While some sites dedicated to Anonymous exist, much of the discussion happens on general discussion boards. Some of their activities are restricted to the Internet, such as disrupting online services that they disagree with through DDoS attacks or by playing pranks, but they have also organized offline protests. Most notably their activism has targeted the Church of Scientology, which has been accused of financially defrauding members and harassing those who leave or criticize the church.

MISUSING INFORMATION

While the Internet facilitates open communication among activists, a dark side exists to this free flow of information: spreading disinformation and confidential material. One such phenomenon is termed the "Human Flesh Search Engine," a loosely knit group of vigilantes mobilized in the chat rooms and forums of China. In one instance, those who expressed unsympathetic and callous opinions about the tragic 2008 Sichuan earthquake, in which tens of thousands of people were killed, were harassed with emails, reported to authorities, and had their personal information published. As a consequence, one individual targeted was arrested and another was threatened with expulsion from school. Similar actions were taken against campaigners for Tibetan independence (even those living outside of China), and their families.

Animal rights activists in the United Kingdom routinely post the personal details of individuals they believe are legitimate targets. In November 2003, when the University of Cambridge was considering building a primate research lab, one group published contact details not only of those involved in animal research, but also a seemingly random collection of individuals from the computing department, including myself. Immediately, my mailbox was overloaded with messages, some polite, others abusive, until I was able to block further ones and the site containing my details was removed. In a separate action, groups of activists intimidated the management of suppliers to an animal testing laboratory, including false claims that they were pedophiles and by sending bomb threats—with the promise that these actions would continue until they shut down their business. In 2009, individuals involved in such intimidation campaigns were jailed, but shortly afterward, the judge who presided over this trial also had his home address published on an Indymedia message board. While this posting was rapidly removed, the server hosting the message board was confiscated and police arrested an administrator.

The power of blogs and forums to allow anyone to become their own media outlet is both a strength and a weakness of the Internet. Topics ignored or suppressed by traditional media can be covered, but new and minor blogs have little to lose should they publish incorrect information. Accordingly, they are often more willing to not confirm their reports and thus to spread disinformation, as was the case with the June 2009 false rumors of accidents at several nuclear power plants in Russia operated by Energoatom. A similar incident in 2007, where rumors were spread via email and SMS, resulted in panic buying of iodine pills and canned food. These are not isolated incidents—the website Snopes.com is filled with the debunking of hoaxes circulated to friends and relatives by well-meaning Internet users. Many are merely pranks, but some have political motivations.

ATTACKING CRITICAL INFRASTRUCTURE

While the Internet allows for intimidation, it cannot directly cause physical harm unless those threats are realized in the offline world. However, as the importance of the Internet in our daily lives grows, the barrier between the online and offline worlds breaks down. The examples so far have shown how an attack on an important website can halt work, how groups can organize anonymously to avoid surveillance, and how private information on the Internet can be leaked or sold. In these cases, the actual harm caused was indirect and the threat required an offline action to cause physical harm to the target. In this final category of attack, I discuss the worrying possibility that activists could interfere with critical infrastructure, causing direct physical harm.

Although activists have not yet used digital technology to cause direct physical harm, nation-states have been carrying out such attacks for some time as part of warfare. We use the term "digital technology" here to encompass the many types of tools and infrastructure that can be used to cause physical harm. In earlier decades, harmful code was loaded directly into a computer through malicious software (malware), today such code is much more likely to arrive over the Internet. In his book, *At the Abyss*, Thomas C. Reed alleged that in 1982 the CIA sabotaged software that monitored a natural gas pipeline that ran through Siberia. This software was programmed to malfunction after a specified period, ultimately causing a large explosion and significant damage. Other cyber-attacks have been carried out as part of military operations. However, these attacks required privileged access before the malware could be introduced (in the pipeline case, the software was tampered with following a tip that it would be stolen by KGB operatives). Similarly, in 2001, a former employee of a water processing plant in Queensland, Australia, used stolen software to release sewage into rivers, killing wildlife.

Nowadays, as more critical infrastructure is connected to the Internet, the need for privileged access is diminishing, opening up vulnerabilities to criminals, terrorists, and activists alike. Indeed, while examples of more recent cyber-attacks remain classified, U.S. government departments have disclosed that they regularly have their computer systems breached by foreign entities, with government intelligence agencies suspected. Given such access, officials believed attackers could seriously disrupt distribution of food and electricity.

For example, in the 2007 Aurora Experiment, security researchers hired by the U.S. government remotely took control of a generator and caused it to shake on its foundations, emit black smoke, and ultimately self-destruct. However, while criminals have the capability to execute these attacks, we have no indication that any are trying. Terrorists, who are less likely to worry about causing harm, already have effective tactics. At the moment, the tools necessary seem unlikely to fall into the hands of activists willing to use them, but it remains a possibility.

Ethical Quandaries: How Activists Justify Destructive Tactics

Throughout this book, we have described some instances of digital activism as constructive and others as destructive. This chapter in particular has made repeated ethical judgments about what constitutes "bad" digital activism. Attributing ethical value is nevertheless difficult because activism often occurs around the world's most controversial and passionately debated political and social issues: rights violations, abuses of power, and even war.

While most readers will view the actions in this chapter as unethical—a DDoS attack on a foreign government, website defacement, or harassment—it is important to acknowledge that the activists themselves believe their tactics to be justified. To give a balanced portrayal of the instances of digital activism, in this section we will look at the different justifications such activists might use for their actions: rejecting the validity of a law, weighing positive over negative effects, and rejecting the ethical legitimacy of the negative effect entirely.

Many of the tactics discussed in this chapter are illegal, especially those that adopt tools and techniques originally developed for criminal purposes. However, many activists do not see the law as a fair measurement of the ethical dimensions of their actions. For example, during the Georgian crisis, Russian activists would likely not respect Georgian laws against the defacement of government websites because these are the laws of a foreign country that the activists see as hostile to their own nation's interests. Members of the Human Flesh Search Engine might also disregard Chinese laws against harassment if they think that the bad acts of the target justified the harassment. Part of the activist identity is to challenge the status quo—this opposition can reach beyond the particular social or political cause the group is fighting to include the laws of the society as well.

A second justification for destructive digital activism is that the negative effect of the action is far less significant than its positive effect. While the animal rights activists in the United Kingdom likely recognized that the publication of a judge's home address would lead to harassment, they probably felt that the intended effect of their action—to dissuade judges from handing out tough sentences to their fellow activists—justified their action. Likewise, even though the activists of Anonymous knew the DDoS attacks of the Church of Scientology website would annoy members and nonmembers of the organization, they likely believed that the greater goal—to stop the church's alleged abuses—justified their action.

One of the most pertinent examples discussed in the context of balancing the positive and negative effects of activism is property damage. What does it matter that a government website is disabled, the participants of the Interfada might have argued, if it demoralizes the enemy and encourages capitulation? DDoS attacks, however, rarely affect only a single targeted website. When a site is disabled by overloading the server on which it is stored, the traffic of all the other sites on that server is also disrupted. Thus, a DDoS attack is likely to damage the accessibility of unrelated sites and will probably incur expenses for parties not linked to the site being targeted. As an extreme case, during the August 2009 DDoS attacks on the Twitter account of Cyxymu, a Georgian blogger, the Twitter micro-blogging site became inaccessible to all of its 30 million users.

The final justification, and the most interesting, is that the destructive act is, in fact, not a bad act at all and thus does not need to be justified. For example, many activists, particularly those with philosophical opposition to modern materialist culture, believe that violence against property (as opposed to violence against people) is not bad. These activists could thus theoretically approve of all the tactics in this chapter that do not cause physical harm to living beings. However, while the ethical cost of property damage may be subjective, the monetary cost is not. For example, the U.S. Department of Defense estimated that it has spent $100 million in taxpayers' money cleaning up after and protecting against cyber incidents.

When justifying a destructive act, activists reject a part of the rationale used to condemn their actions. They may reject the validity of the law that finds their action illegal, the premise that the negative effect of the action outweighed any benefit, or the position that the act is destructive at all. Activism often exists in opposition to the power structures that govern ethics within societies, so it is important to judge each action on its merit rather than simply accept the determinations of those in power.

Conclusion

Looking forward, the effectiveness of destructive digital activism is likely to grow as we rely on the Internet more and more in our daily lives. And, despite the inevitable lag, law enforcement's ability to catch and prosecute digital activists will also increase. Just as the tools used by activists are often driven by criminal innovation, the experience and legislative support law enforcement gains as it investigates cybercrime will help agencies track down digital activists, making such tactics a less attractive option. Technological improvements will also help resist attacks. Today, criminals and activists are often able to circumvent existing protections, but this could change. Whether we see these advances as positive or negative depends on whether we believe the initial act was justified. While these advances would help the victims of harassment, they would also remove an avenue for protest that many consider legitimate.

PART 3

Effects: What Is Digital Activism's Value?

```
01111001
01101111
01110101
01110010
01110111
01101111
01110010
01101100
01100100
01110100
01101111
01100011
01101000
01100001
01101110
01100111
01100101
```

Measuring the Success of Digital Campaigns

Dave Karpf

The digital revolution has provided us with an expansive set of tools for pursuing activist campaigns. Never before have the powers of self-publishing in video, audio, or written format been so widely accessible to so many. Anyone with an Internet connection has a platform for getting the word out. But do these new tactics and platforms make our attempts at political activism any more *successful* than before? If a half million people sign an online petition to end poverty, reduce global warming emissions, or overthrow a repressive regime, what effect does that actually have? Digital activism boasts a wide array of tools, but in many ways they only make the measurement of success that much more difficult. This chapter focuses on two different types of metrics used in digital activism: tactical and strategic. Tactical measurements count the number of signatures, visits, blog posts, etc. They provide indicators of how many individuals have taken some action related to your campaign. Strategic metrics, on the other hand, measure success. They require a clear theory of how you expect your tactics to make a difference, in turn clarifying which measures actually contribute to a win or a loss.

The difference between these two types of measurement dates to the analog era. I first became interested in the difference between them during a campus environmental rally at Oberlin

College in Ohio. The organizers had spent months preparing and they managed to gather a large crowd of students to hear speakers, hold placards, and demonstrate their support for the protection of a West Coast forest. Tactically, the event was a great success, one that the group leaders were rightly proud of. But since the fate of the forest was to be decided by the California state government—2,349 miles away—any strategic measure of the event would have had to find it lacking. The students chanted loudly that day, but since Ohio is so far from California, not nearly loud enough to be heard by the state government! In the digital age, the Internet provides every one of us with a megaphone. But, as with those college students, whether the right people will hear and react to digital activism is a more complicated matter.

Successful activist campaigns have always come down to a set of people mobilizing the resources at their disposal to either affect the choices of powerful decision makers or to replace those actors with others more attuned to the beliefs and preferences of the people. To accomplish this goal, activists use the tools at their disposal to educate their fellow citizens and mobilize pressure tactics. But, online or offline, large or small, mainstream or radical, success in all forms of activism must be judged at the strategic, rather than the tactical, level. And, while the availability of online engagement platforms leads to a slew of tactical data, it can also make measurement of success all the more difficult. In the examples that follow, I will discuss some of the pitfalls embedded in easy-to-find tactical-level measures available online, as well as offer a few lessons on how to construct strategic metrics of success in the digital age.

Netroots or Astroturf? How Many Twitter Followers Until the Revolution Occurs?

Twitter is the most recent social media service to arrive on the international scene. With roughly forty-six million visitors per day and more than seventy million members, it has been hailed as a major expansion on SMS messaging services. Twitter users can choose who they would like to "follow," and post micro-blog updates of up to 140 characters that are viewable to their own "followers." Supporting applications such as the bit.ly service, which converts Web addresses into a small number of characters so they can be embedded in a Twitter update, help to make the service an essential medium for spreading messages and forwarding blog posts, articles, pictures, and videos to your extended network. Hashtags (#phrase) added to these messages allow users to search for posts about a given topic; frequently discussed hashtags appear on the front page of the website as "trending topics." Twitter posts currently receive a particularly high clickthrough rate, indicating that those messages that are sent out to your network are often actually read—a rarity in an online information landscape where attention is perhaps the scarcest commodity of all.

At the tactical level, Twitter offers a few readily identifiable metrics of success. The first and most obvious is number of followers. The only people who will see your tweets are those who are following you. Therefore, the more followers you have, the more influence you can potentially wield. Second is re-tweets—if you say something insightful or funny over Twitter, your followers might forward it to their followers, generally with an added header such as "RT @davekarpf" (the @ sign indicates a Twitter user and is hyperlinked to his or her profile page). Re-tweets amplify your message and can lead to additional followers. A third simple metric is total number of tweets. Many Twitter accounts remain dormant for weeks or months, their users either ignoring the system or reading but not responding themselves. Other users will tweet constantly throughout the day. While there is such a thing as "too much" (and this can lead to people "unfollowing" you), the more influential users are likely to be those who tweet more often.

So more followers, more tweets, and more re-tweets are all good. What does this mean for measuring success in digital activism? Is a digital activist with five thousand followers more successful than one with fifty? If we Twitter and get re-tweeted often enough, will that actually accomplish our goals? The answer, of course, is that it all depends on what you are trying to accomplish in your campaign.

Consider the rise of "Top Conservatives on Twitter" (#TCOT), a hashtag created to group American Twitter users of the political right. Conservative political strategist Michael Patrick Leahy launched this website in the aftermath of the 2008 presidential election that saw Democrat Barack Obama elected to office. Leahy's website was used by prominent Republican leaders to boast about their number of Twitter followers and was regularly cited as evidence that Republicans were "building a new conservative community" online. Competitors for the position of Republican National Committee chairman boasted about their number of Twitter followers, while Republican representative John Culberson went so far as to say that the technology is "the next revolution that's going to take back the Congress." As conservative leaders in America gained more Twitter followers than their progressive rivals, the argument has been made that this is a sign of their reemergence.

While it is never a good idea to *underestimate* the power of a new medium, this rampant optimism about tactical measures should give us pause. Winning national elections requires the persuasion and mobilization of millions of people. Those who are likely to follow a candidate on Twitter are already active supporters. Those who need to be persuaded often are not even using the medium and certainly aren't following elite conservative politicians. The same can be said for many activist campaigns. Twitter can be an excellent means for communicating within a community of networked activists and, as such, can be a valuable means of spreading the word about an upcoming event, important news item, or memorable observation. But if major social or political changes could be accomplished merely by communicating with like-minded peers, such outcomes would be much easier to accomplish than they actually are. Successful political activism is *hard*, much harder than the tactical metrics would lead us to believe.

Complicating the matter even further is an essential and unfortunate reality of digital activism: the tactic-level data are almost always suspect. Any metric of influence that is related to financial incentives becomes the target of manipulation by skilled coders seeking to game the system. In the blogosphere, for instance, hyperlinks are frequently used to identify top blogs, and this has given rise to "splogs"—spam-blogs that are set up as phantom sites to artificially boost hyperlink levels. Similarly, Web traffic measures can be gamed by computer programs. On Twitter, dozens of services offer to increase a user's follower base by 500 or 5,000 in a matter of days . . . for a price. Of course, these additional followers are essentially useless. I could set up 1,000 Twitter accounts myself if I had the time and inclination—it is entirely free and takes very little time. These additional followers are ghosts, however. They do not read, clickthrough, take action, or re-tweet. They serve to distort the tactical metrics in the hopes of boosting revenues for outside actors. Unfortunately for the digital activist, an endless battle is constantly under way between malicious code-writers and spammers trying to game any social media site for profit and the host site's code-writers trying to counter them with filters and other protective measures. In the midst of this firefight, we should generally remain cautious about putting too much faith in any single metric of digital influence.

All of this is not meant to discourage use of new media in activist campaigns. Rather, digital activists must be clear about the strategic goals they are pursuing and identify the relevant data accordingly. In one recent example, the *Washington Post* produced an online video segment on its site; "Mouthpiece Theater" was meant to provide entertaining off-the-cuff political commentary from two of its reporters, Dana Milbank and Chris Cillizza. On

Friday, July 31, 2009, the video included some remarks about Sec. of State Hillary Clinton that many digital activists found to be sexist and deeply offensive. Within hours, these networked activists organized a "twitterbomb"—gathering a large set of users to simultaneously flood the *Post* with outraged comments over Twitter. Blog posts and YouTube videos were quickly produced as well, and these same online activists spread the word throughout their networks of followers about these items. The strategic theory here was simple enough: the *Post* was producing these videos in an attempt to appeal to the small segment of the public that would *want* to watch video of a couple of political reporters every week. If digital activists (who make up much of that public) loudly complained, the *Post* would be likely to realize its error and respond. Indeed, the offending video was removed within hours, both reporters apologized for their remarks, and within a week "Mouthpiece Theater" was cancelled. The relevant metric for this brief digital activist campaign was the number of participants in the twitterbomb. It becomes clearly identifiable only when placed within a strategic framework.

When in Doubt, Blend: The Blogosphere Authority Index as an Alternate Path

Strategic metrics must be designed within the context of an activist campaign. Tactical metrics, though abundantly available, can be misleading. For those academics and observers interested in digital activism but not operating from within a campaign, this presents a challenge: the best data are often kept closely guarded by campaigns and organizations—the tremendously successful Obama campaign, for instance, holds much of the information about "what worked" as a closely guarded secret. If we can't judge Twitter influence directly by follower counts, Facebook strength by friend totals, or blog authority by hyperlinks alone, how are we to measure much of anything in the emerging world of digital politics?

The solution I generally recommend is to minimize errors by blending various types of data. One such effort is the Blogosphere Authority Index (BAI), a system that provides monthly rankings of the top 25 progressive and conservative U.S. political blogs. I crafted the BAI after noticing that earlier academic studies of the blogosphere relied too heavily on faulty data sources and failed to provide any measure of which blogs were the largest and most influential. That, in turn, led to questions about how we are to define "influence" in political blogging. In a 2008 article for the Institute for Politics, Democracy, and the Internet's *Politics and Technology Review*, I described the problem as follows:

> Consider the following example: blogger A posts infrequently on her personal site. This results in a small reader base, and comparatively few hypertext links from around the blogosphere. Years ago, blogger A was a mentor to bloggers B, C, and D, and she now holds a key position within her party's establishment. The few people who frequent her blog are highly influential, either in the blogosphere or in more traditional political institutions. Blogger B posts once or twice a day on his individual blog, which was picked up by a major online news magazine last year. He has a journalistic background and specializes in developing new arguments or breaking new stories. He chooses to be a blogger because he likes to set his own deadlines, operate without an editor looking over his shoulder, and publish instantaneously. He often relies on blogger A for insights and tidbits that he researches and turns into original articles. He is among the most often cited bloggers online, by liberals and conservatives alike. Blogger C posts 15–20 times per day. She rarely publishes original content, instead pouring over other blogs and writing short, pithy posts that tell her reader base about something interesting elsewhere on the web. She acts as a gatekeeper for her gigantic readership, who use her site as a roadmap to the rest of the Internet. Blogger D is the purveyor of one of the most active community blogs

in the country. He posts 8 times per day, with some original content and some "open threads" so that his community can keep their own discussion going. This community also publishes their own diaries, often 50 or so in a day. Political endorsements from this site mean dollars in a candidate's pocket. The membership recently spun off two new sites to support activity around universal health care and global warming, and the policy proposals from these sites have been adopted into Congressional legislation. *Which blogger is the most influential?*

The point of this passage is to indicate that "influence," "power," and "success" in online media can have a variety of meanings. Rather than selecting one measure of influence, the BAI identifies a different metric for each of the four types listed above: tracking "blogroll"-mentions, hyperlinks, site traffic, and total volume of comments per week. (A "blogroll" is a list of like-minded bloggers offered as a sidebar on most blogs. Services such as Technorati track the total number of hyperlinks between blogs, while services such as Sitemeter track site traffic). Each of these measures has its own limitations, but by converting them to rankings and then combining them, we develop a much more comprehensive picture of the top political blogs. This same methodology of drawing upon networked data and blending various sources can be applied to Twitter, Facebook, or other social Web spaces. It reduces many of the biases that result from depending on a single unreliable data source and lets us speak generally about the online individuals or activist communities that are developing political strength in an increasingly networked society.

While the BAI serves as a valuable tool for academic research, it remains anchored in tactic-level metrics. The system can tell us which political blogs gained influence during the 2008 election and which ones lost influence—but that tells us relatively little about the strategic-level question of "Were their campaigns successful?" For an example of such strategic-level metrics, I will now turn to a short-term campaign organized by the DailyKos. com blogging community.

Online Impacts We Can Feel: Moneybombing the Electoral Landscape

On October 17, 2008, Republican representative Michele Bachmann appeared on the political news program *Hardball with Chris Matthews* as a surrogate for John McCain during McCain's presidential campaign. Bachmann, an outspoken conservative, argued that Barack Obama's relationships with various left-wing individuals should give voters pause and suggested that he might hold "anti-American views." As the host of the program pressed her on what she meant by this claim, Bachmann went a step too far, suggesting that she wished "the American media would take a great look at the views of the people in Congress and find out, are they pro-America or anti-America?" Such a statement raised the specter of a dark chapter in American history—the Red Scare of the 1950s, which sought to root out communist sympathizers through high-profile politicized hearings and blacklists of supposed sympathizers.

The Bachmann episode was immediately picked up by outraged progressive bloggers and was placed on YouTube, where it received 200,000 views. This, if considered in isolation, would be an excellent example of a tactical success and strategic failure. Bachmann was running for reelection in Minnesota's 6th Congressional District. Only the voters of her district have the power to hold her accountable, the rest of the nation, indeed the rest of the world, are merely spectators. The strategic targets in electoral campaigns are voters—either supportive voters who need to be mobilized or undecided voters who need to be persuaded. If digital activists living outside a congressional district wish to affect an election, they must find some means of translating their wishes into resources that can affect these targets.

In this case, online progressive activists, also called the "netroots"—and the DailyKos blogging community in particular—were clearly aware of this strategic imperative and acted accordingly. The "kossacks" immediately set up an online fund-raising page at the Democratic fund-raising portal ActBlue.com and started sending donations to Bachmann's opponent, the little-known Elwyn Tinklenberg. The progressive bloggers embedded video clips of Bachmann's statement, drew clear parallels with the era of McCarthyism, and asked their readers to send a clear message by donating to Tinklenberg. In less than forty-eight hours, more than $840,000 was raised online to support Tinklenberg—nearly as much as the candidate had raised over the course of the previous *year.* This netroots "moneybomb" attracted local and national media attention as well, keeping Bachmann's misstatement in the news and forcing citizens in her district to consider whether they were comfortable with her.

Bachmann was reelected, albeit the race was much closer than she had anticipated. What is important to note in this example is the analytic value that results from having a clear sense of strategic targeting. Dozens of tactic-level metrics could have been applied to such a campaign: YouTube video views, blog posts, hyperlinks, blog comments, media mentions, etc. In the digital environment, it can be easy to get lost in the noise of these metrics. A strategic statement identifies the signal within all this noisy data. The DailyKos community sought to affect a congressional election. Since they are an international community-of-interest, they had to overcome a geographic hurdle: unless they themselves lived in Minnesota's 6th District or personally knew voters who did, what could they do? They decided that they could make a difference by mobilizing tens of thousands of small donors, nearly doubling the local candidate's budget overnight and leading to further media attention that, in turn, would be noticed by residents of the district. In this case, the two *metrics of success* were money raised and mainstream media coverage. The bloggers used a suite of digital tactics to achieve these strategic objectives (tactics that would have been impossible in an analog era), but the actual measures of success can be limited to these two because these were the vehicles by which a diffuse community-of-interest could affect the outcome of a geographically sited election.

Strategic Metrics from the Global Perspective

The examples thus far have come from the United States—my area both of personal experience and academic expertise. Digital activism, however, is frequently *global* in scope. How do tactical and strategic metrics change when applied to other countries and international campaigns?

My colleague David Faris at the University of Pennsylvania has conducted substantial research on the use of digital media in Egypt. He has found that the Egyptian citizenry, despite relatively low Internet-adoption rates, can be strongly influenced by political bloggers. To paraphrase his work, the key has lain in cultivating relationships with the independent media and in engaging in four types of activity that *augment* the media establishment: (1) breaking stories that otherwise would have been overlooked, (2) documenting stories with unique textual, photographic, or video evidence, (3) transmitting stories to a global audience, and (4) "red-lining," in which blog activists speak about topics that are officially off-limits to the Egyptian media. Many of these activities are hard to identify using the tactical metrics most prevalent in the United States—traffic rankings and hyperlink analysis do not highlight these important accomplishments—but Faris uses in-depth interviews and case analysis to highlight how the Internet is affecting that nation. He finds that Egyptian bloggers have broken major stories on sexual harassment in the streets of Cairo, documented the persecution of Sudanese refugees, broadcast police brutality stories that otherwise would have gone ignored, and spoken up about the Egyptian military when the newspapers could not. Time and again, a small set of Egyptian digital activists has coordinated activities to alter government actions in substantive ways.

This once again highlights the importance of applying a strategic logic to the design of any metric of digital activism. Cross-national comparison can be difficult both because different countries have varying levels of Internet access and also because the power structures in different nations can be radically divergent. New technologies offer an expansive suite of tools for engaging our fellow citizens, but some forms of engagement are more effective than others. Would an America-based blog with one million visits have more impact in Egypt than an Egyptian blog whose five hundred visitors were all key journalists or fellow digital activists? Seems unlikely. Tactical metrics, then, are only truly impressive when placed in context. The actions that are most likely to be successful in the United Kingdom are not the same as those that will succeed in Saudi Arabia. Measures of success are not as simple as "How many people signed our online petition?" Rather, they require an understanding of the existing power structure and a theory of change that explains how a given activist campaign is intended to affect that structure. Only once those conditions have been satisfied can the key metrics of success be identified.

The Principles of Organizing Applied to the Digital World

In thinking about strategic metrics, then, it is important to consider some of the classic concepts in activist campaigning. Famed Harvard professor and longtime labor organizer Marshall Ganz explains strategy as follows: "Strategy is about turning 'what you have' into 'what you need' to get 'what you want'—how to turn resources into power . . . Strategic action is a way of acting, not an alternative to acting. It is acting with intentionality and mindfulness of one's goals, as opposed to acting out of habit or impulse." That concept of strategy can be traced back to Sun Tzu's *The Art of War*, and I would suggest to you that the rise of digital activism primarily affects only the first part: "what you have." Digital communication tools provide us with a wealth of new opportunities for mobilizing our resources and turning them into power. Decades ago, very few people had their own power of the printing press; today an Internet connection gives you the power to self-publish.

Metrics of success, meanwhile, can perhaps be best understood as the second part of Ganz's formulation: "what you need." Activist campaigns in any locale across the globe seek to mobilize power, and this mobilization can and should be quantified. It is not simply measured by hyperlinks or clickrates, though. Identifying *what to measure* only becomes clear once we have figured out which actions (and in what quantities) a digital activist campaign seeks to encourage and pursue. How many online petition signatures are necessary to achieve a certain goal? Will change be accomplished by a broad outpouring of shallow support or by accessing and convincing one key individual? Either or both of these can be appropriate. Measurement can only happen after the question has been answered, however.

And, of course, digital activist campaigns will operate and be measured differently depending on variation in the third part of the formulation: "what you want." Overthrowing a corrupt and violent political regime requires different tools from passing a local recycling initiative. The digital revolution affects the range of tools available to both campaigns and brings with it a wealth of tactic-level data that can be used to judge either. Students of political change and the Internet must remain clear-eyed when evaluating this data, however, because the numbers tell us little in the absence of a strategic logic.

Conclusion

The digital revolution provides social change proponents with a dizzying array of tools. Between the heightened power of self-publishing, networked activist campaigns, crowd-sourced information gathering, and viral messages, the digital era offers almost *too many* metrics. The central aim of this chapter has been to introduce and explain the difference between the tactical and strategic levels of measurement. Tactical measurements are the simple traffic numbers: Facebook friends, Twitter followers, blog posts, video views, e-petition signatures. They can be impressive in their own right, but also can easily mislead. This is particularly the case because many of the most easy-to-obtain metrics are, themselves, of questionable quality. Any metric that is used to help monetize a system—traffic levels, hyperlinks, etc.—is likely to be the subject of fierce competition between spammers or hackers seeking to distort the numbers for personal gain and code-writers attempting to counter their efforts.

Separating the "signal" from the "noise" in online metrics of success can best be achieved by focusing attention on the strategic level of activity. The essence of strategy lies in answering the Ganz question: How does an activist group intend to turn "what they have" into "what they need" to get "what they want"? Or, put another way, the strategic level asks, "How do we expect to win, and how will we know that we're achieving it?" The examples above illustrate a variety of answers to this strategic question, and each example illustrates the importance of a distinct type of data. For academics and observers seeking to understand broader comparative trends, reliance is often placed on aggregate tactical data—the Blogosphere Authority Index serves as one example of how such efforts can be constructed. Where the strategic logic of a digital activism effort is unclear or unknown, remaining agnostic about which tactic-level data source is most valuable is usually best, with merging several types a surer route to clear understanding. In essence, strategy tells us what data to look at, and, in the absence of strategy, we are best off blending and looking at a bit of everything.

The New Casualties: Prisons and Persecution

Simon Columbus

When the Iranian authorities arrested Sina Motallebi in 2003 for criticizing the government in his blog and speaking with foreign journalists, the young Iranian blogosphere was alarmed. Repressive regimes have always moved to silence those who express themselves freely—so what made this arrest more shocking than earlier arrests of those critical of the regime? Motallebi's arrest was one of the first instances of a growing trend in the political persecution of bloggers, and a direct challenge to the cyber-utopianism of the 1990s. Although the Internet allows activists greater access to the tools of mass communication and coordination, it does not protect them from persecution.

The Internet initially carried the promise of a space for free expression and communication, where individuals and groups from all over the globe could voice their opinions and concerns to a worldwide audience. This ideal was exemplified by the Declaration of the Independence of Cyberspace, penned in 1996 by John Perry Barlow, a respected Internet theorist and a founding member of the Electronic Frontier Foundation. In it, Barlow declared the Internet free from the restriction and repression of offline political spaces:

Governments of the Industrial World . . . I declare the global social space we are building to be naturally independent of the tyrannies you seek to impose on us. You have no moral right to rule us nor do you possess any methods of enforcement we have true reason to fear. Governments derive their just powers from the consent of the governed. You have neither solicited nor received ours. We did not invite you. . . . Cyberspace does not lie within your borders. . . . We are creating a world where anyone, anywhere may express his or her beliefs, no matter how singular, without fear of being coerced into silence or conformity.

This was the promise of a new frontier open to those who crossed into it first. But just as the Wild West has today come under the rule of law, the Internet was soon targeted by law enforcement officials. Now, although we are mostly free to visit sites run by citizens of all nations, governments decide what we are allowed to see and, more important, to create. Motallebi's arrest signaled the end of an era of political promise for bloggers in Iran and in other countries as well. It was one of the first signs that the Web was not detached from the politics of real life but intimately connected with it.

In this chapter, I will use my own research to analyze arrests of bloggers, from Sina Motallebi's arrest on April 23, 2003, through August 1, 2009. Although bloggers are not the only digital activists, I consider them reasonably representative of political Internet users, thus allowing me to discern general patterns of persecution of digital activists of all stripes.

Creating a Charge to Fit the Crime

Between 2003 and 2009, 30 countries arrested 161 bloggers a total of 202 times.[1] (The number of digital activists arrested during these seven years is, of course, even higher.) Not all of the blogger arrests can be called "political"—in some cases, bloggers violated laws, e.g., copyright, or committed libel against individuals or corporations. But the majority of arrests do have a clear political motive—in 162 of 202 cases, bloggers were persecuted for political reasons.

In most cases, the real reasons for political arrests are kept secret. Often, detained political activists are never brought to court and tried. In my research, I found that of 202 bloggers arrested, only 37 were brought to trial and sentenced judicially. While the actual number of sentences might be higher, either because detainees are sentenced in secret or because a sentence does not attract much attention, it can be assumed that most of those arrested were never intended to go to trial. That being the case, determining what specific action of a digital activist led to the arrest is almost impossible. In countries that lack a functioning (or independent) legal system, the attention of those in power is often attracted, not by one discrete deed, but by consistent and growing political activity.

If the authorities publicize a reason for an arrest, it may well be bogus. When the Vietnam government had Nguyen Van Hai arrested in April 2008, prosecutors charged him with tax evasion. Hai is a member of a group of bloggers known as the Union of Independent Journalists. The group had called for protests along the route of the torch for the 2008 Beijing Olympic Games when it passed through Ho Chi Minh City. The goal was to bring attention to Chinese human rights abuses. Hai, himself, had featured reports about similar protests around the world on his blog. While Hai was almost certainly arrested for his political activities, the charges brought against him did not involve politics.

Most governments, however, do not make use of such sophisticated tactics to silence bloggers they view as offensive. In nearly every country that persecutes bloggers and other digital activists, laws restrict a broad range of expression. Most countries outlaw sedition, while some limit libeling politicians or religion. Some also restrict hate speech.

One typical charge is that the blogger advocated the overthrow of or was engaged in actions to overthrow the state or current regime. This charge is used especially in countries where criticism of the leader is explicitly or implicitly forbidden—China or Iran, for example. Such laws, which often allow very long prison sentences, can be easily used to lock up activists for years.

Another common charge is espionage. Iran has repeatedly accused digital activists of cooperation with foreign nations, especially the United States. Such a charge carries both a long prison sentence and also places a heavy moral burden on the person accused.

Yet another charge often hurled at activists is libel. Kareem Amer, the first Egyptian blogger to be sentenced, was charged with libeling both Pres. Hosni Mubarak and Islam. This claim was true in his case, but nevertheless used as an excuse to silence a political activist rather than to protect the president's reputation and prevent criticism of Islam.

Accusations of libel and defamation are raised in about 10 percent of detentions of bloggers. Besides Iran, Malaysia and Morocco are among the countries that most use libel as a charge. These countries use anti-defamation laws to respond to attacks on politicians at a national or local level. In Morocco, criticizing the king or the royal family is illegal. Accordingly, most libel cases are brought against activists who dare to speak out against the king or his politics. In Malaysia, a country where power is highly decentralized, accusations of libel usually come from local politicians who have been, in their opinion, defamed by a blog entry.

Many countries also have laws prohibiting hate speech. European hate speech laws are often aimed at preventing the circulation of right-wing propaganda. In some countries, denying the Holocaust can result in imprisonment (although few have been charged under these laws recently).

In East Asian countries, Singapore or Malaysia, for example, hate speech laws are intended to forestall conflicts between different ethnicities. Singapore has repeatedly arrested individuals for posting racist remarks on the Internet; Malaysia has used its hate speech laws to persecute one of its most prolific critical bloggers, Raja Petra Kamarudin, on charges that he criticized Islam and the Prophet Mohammed on his blog, thus insulting Muslims.

Moneyed Interests

The harassment or arrest of activists for Internet-based political campaigns is the core study of this chapter. Antigovernment action is not the only risky behavior engaged in by digital activists, however. Whistle-blowers and activists exposing the wrongdoing of corporations are constantly at risk of being sued. Especially in Western countries, where copyright and trademark laws are strong, infringement of these laws has often been used against whistle-blowers.

In many cases, the legal expenses alone make mounting a defense (a court case can go through several appeals) impossible for bloggers or activists; they are, accordingly, forced to remove their posts. Where the law does not provide corporations with a legal means of silencing their critics, corruption and cronyism can still deny activists justice. In January 2009, an Egyptian court fined Mohammed Mabrouk for blogging about environmental pollution by, and working conditions at, a chemical company. In a sentence called "overly harsh" and "an unacceptable violation of freedom of expression" by the Arab Network for Human Rights Information, Mabrouk was ordered to pay a fine of about US$450 plus more than US$7200 in compensation to the company he allegedly libeled. Activists who commit themselves to environmental or workers' issues are especially vulnerable to the strength of entangled economic and political interests.

Generally, arrests based on attacks on powerful economic interests are most likely to be made by the local police. Arrests that take into account, or are solely based on, an activist belonging to a group that challenges the status quo are more usually directed by security forces at the national level.

Targeted Groups

The above examples clearly show that the reasons given and those actually behind an arrest are rarely identical. In general, I propose to differentiate two patterns of arrests. Pattern one is arrests of individuals in response to a specific action; pattern two is the detentions of activists affiliated with some kind of group. Both patterns are common, though pattern two is most common in countries under authoritarian rule.

I would like to distinguish four different kinds of targeted groups: political parties, civil rights movements, religions, and ethnic minorities. While affiliations with these groups are not mutually exclusive—because no clear line exists between parties and movements or those who belong to both ethnic and religious minorities—some distinctions about their treatment can be made.

POLITICAL PARTIES

Egypt has a strong culture of digital activism, with some of the most impressive uses of digital technologies for political opposition originating there. But the Egyptian regime also has a long history of repressing political parties and has never shied away from arresting even the most prominent cyber-dissidents.

Many of the country's digital activists are either members of the Islamist Muslim Brotherhood or one of the liberal parties that make up the Kefaya coalition. Bloggers and digital activists associated with the Muslim Brotherhood, by far the largest opposition party in Parliament, are special targets and are regularly harassed and detained.

CIVIL RIGHTS MOVEMENTS

In Iran, a country that has seen even more repression of digital activists than Egypt, authorities target civil rights movements. Iran has a strong women's rights movement that in the past was vocal in its support of the One Million Signatures campaign, a bid to promote women's rights in the Islamic Republic. Members of the loosely affiliated group of organizers behind the campaign have repeatedly been arrested by the Iranian authorities.

RELIGIOUS GROUPS

Religious discrimination is particularly concentrated in Islamic countries, where evangelizing for any other religion or converting to another religion is often considered to be a crime. Saudi Arabia, in particular, has repeatedly arrested individuals who posted online about their conversion to Christianity; similar instances can be found in Iran. Egypt, where Copts make up more than 10 percent of the population, has repeatedly arrested members of this ancient branch of Christianity.

Atheist bloggers and activists, too, have been victims of persecution in many places. Again, they are most at risk in Islamic countries. When atheist Kareem Amer, the first blogger to be sentenced in Egypt, was sent to prison for four years, three of those years were given for "defamation of Islam." Other nonbelieving activists throughout the Arab world have also been imprisoned, many of them from the Islamic Republic of Iran.

But belonging to a particular religious group is not the only reason for government repression of digital activists. China has repeatedly arrested those who reported on marginalized religious groups such as the Roman Catholic underground church.

ETHNIC MINORITIES

China has also been at the forefront of repression of minority activists. In the spring of 2008, just before the Olympic Games in Beijing, China was quick to respond to riots in Tibet. The communist government cracked down on some of the most remarkable Tibetan voices on the Internet. China has done the same to Uighur activists (who, as Muslims, also belong to a religious minority).

China is not the only country that moves to persecute ethnic minority activists in times of unrest. Egypt's second-longest serving blogger at the moment is Musaad Abu Fagr, a prominent Bedouin activist from the Sinai who was arrested after riots erupted at a demonstration against the government. In fact, he was not directly involved in the demonstration—the only connection was his prominence as an advocate for Bedouin rights.

Elsewhere, arrests of ethnic minority activists are made within the context of a continuing struggle. Iran and other countries of the Middle East have repeatedly arrested Kurdish bloggers, some of them advocates of an independent Kurdistan. Detentions of separatists and activists are, of course, always highly political; both their ethnicity and their political stance put them in danger.

Citizen Leaders

"Twitter revolutions"—uprisings instigated through the use of digital technologies—have led to another category of arrest. Because social media-powered activism does not need strong hierarchies, governments often have trouble finding a campaign's leaders. When citizen leaders do rise to prominence, they are often persecuted. For example, on April 6, 2008, workers in the Egyptian textile industry went on strike, attracting a lot of attention. A Facebook group started by Esraa Abdel Fattah called for a nationwide general strike in solidarity with the workers and was one way information about the workers' grievances and the strike itself was disseminated. Prior to the date of the strike, Egyptian authorities, fearing that the unrest would spread, had started to arrest activists who supported the workers. "The police simply arrested people they knew as they had no exact information as to who was behind the disturbances," noted the journalism advocacy organization Reporters Without Borders, "The authorities do not know who is behind this protest because it was launched on the Internet. So they are cracking down on anyone who may have issued the strike call, and bloggers are likely suspects."

Authorities do not readily understand nonhierarchical forms of organization. A spontaneous "flashmob" is almost inconceivable to them. Therefore, the average citizen starting a group that could possibly participate in action against those in charge soon becomes subject to state repression. In the state's eyes, a leader must be found, and authorities either identify somebody like Esraa Abdel Fattah as that leader or, if authorities realize that they cannot locate a leader, a random individual is arrested as a substitute or scapegoat.

Forms of Persecution

Arrests are not the only form of persecution; in many cases, government officials intimidate activists through harassment, which can range from phone calls and insulting or threatening comments on blog posts to visits at the home or workplace of an activist. Authorities threaten to harm not only the activist, but also his or her family, to try to silence critical voices.

Many regimes restrict the international travel of both online and offline activists. China has repeatedly refused to let critics leave the country to receive awards, while Saudi Arabia has put a general travel ban on many of that country's activists. Some activists, returning home from abroad, have been held at airports for hours and often have their personal belongings, especially their laptops and memory devices, confiscated.

Activists have also been summoned to police stations. In China, this practice has become known as "being invited for tea." Once at the station, a person is held for hours. My research has found that approximately one in seven arrests did not last longer than a single day. Most of these short arrests are actually aimed at intimidating activists: in only a very few cases was a blogger called in to account for an actual deed. One who was, however, was Savva Terentyev, a Russian youth who in a blog comment called for public burnings of corrupt policemen, though he never committed a physical act of violence. Terentyev was summoned to appear at the police station, although the police required few other activists to appear. (He was later formally charged and convicted of inciting enmity and publicly humiliating representatives of a social group.)

Bloggers in Prison

My research shows that the average time a blogger spends in prison is 87 days, and we can safely assume that other digital activists are treated similarly. It is interesting to note that arrest and incarceration figures vary significantly. In 2003, Sina Motallebi was not only the first but also the only blogger to be arrested. In the following years, the number of bloggers arrested has risen. However, 2008 saw fewer new arrests (39) than in 2007 (44). Because of the number of long-term prisoners, however, 2008 was the year in which more bloggers than ever before were in prison. A total of 61 individuals—4 more than in 2007—spent some time behind bars within those 12 months.

Long-term prisoners who sometimes have been in jail for years, significantly affect the statistics, skewing the average up. If we remove those who were still in jail as of August 1, 2009, the average jail term for bloggers sinks drastically—from 87 to 32 days. Clearly, a small group of detained bloggers experiences the extreme hardship of extended incarceration. On August 1, 2009, at least 14 bloggers had already been in jail for more than a year and were still awaiting their release.

Countries that detain bloggers most frequently do not necessarily detain them for long periods. A look at the data from the three countries that repress bloggers the most—China, Egypt, and Iran—demonstrates this. In China and Egypt, approximately one-third of arrests last less than one week. In Iran, I have not recorded any arrest that lasted only one day, but one in six detained bloggers was released after less than a week. Hossein Derakhshan, the imprisoned "Blogfather" of Iranian blogging, is an anomaly in that he has been in prison for more than a year as of this writing.

The effectiveness of these detentions in deterring critical bloggers differs from country to country. In China, one out of five people identified in my research has been arrested more than once. In Egypt, every third person arrested is a repeat offender. In Iran, on the other hand, only 10 percent of those arrested have been in prison more than once during the time they were writing their blog. In Iran, popular awareness of the treatment of political prisoners may be a crucial tactic in effectively deterring opposition bloggers and reducing repeat arrests. Iran's prisons are well known for their bad conditions and claims of torture are frequent. Most political prisoners—and thus also detained digital activists—are held in the infamous Evin prison. The first blogger to die in jail was imprisoned in Evin—Omid Reza Mir Sayafi died on March 18, 2009, apparently after being denied medical attention.

But horrible conditions and torture are not exclusive to Iran. Video blogger Wael Abbas has been harassed for exposing torture in Egyptian prisons, and Kareem Amer is reported to have been beaten several times in jail. In many countries, arrested activists are facing systematic attacks on their health and life.

Iran regularly charges arrested activists exorbitant bail, a practice not dissimilar to ransom. Sums of US$100,000 and greater are usual. To raise such large amounts, the whole family must contribute; thus the blogger free on bail is under great obligation to cease blogging and remain in the country while awaiting trial. Often, activists receive suspended sentences, which can be seen as another bid to curtail future activities.

In China, individuals are not detained but are often put under house arrest or held in some alternative facility. Hu Jia, a Chinese human rights advocate and blogger, had been held at his house for months prior to his arrest on December 27, 2007. One man, He Weihua, was forcibly confined to a psychiatric clinic the same year—after he published investigative reports and ignored a warning when Chinese authorities raided his home and confiscated his laptop.

In He's case, his family at least knew what happened to him. Sometimes, people just vanish. Chen Qitang had been detained for more than a year without trial. When his wife called the court to inquire about him, she learned that her husband had been sentenced to two and a half years in prison nearly one week before.

Countermeasures

Unreliable judicial systems make it impossible for digital activists to be sure that their actions are within the law. Even where authorities respect national laws, those laws may not include human and civil rights protections; they may also restrict freedom of expression and leave little room for activism. I have written a great deal about what states do to limit activism, but online activists have found three ways to avoid persecution: anonymity, fame, and the use of campaigns.

ANONYMITY

Anonymity is the principal way online activists avoid persecution. Activists can protect their anonymity by posting under a pseudonym, using a proxy Web browser that hides the IP address of their computer, encrypting data that are stored or transmitted from their computer, and never revealing personal information online. While these measures can help achieve a high level of anonymity, absolute safety can never be achieved as governments are becoming more and more sophisticated in tracking the movements of their citizens online. In addition, some are offline as well as online activists. They use the Internet as a tool but are also out on the street, where their actions are directly observable by law enforcement agents.

Anonymity can harm an activist's credibility. Especially for someone fighting for a political ideal, putting his or her own name on the ideas being discussed and the actions being encouraged is important. Some anonymous bloggers have won high credibility: The Thai blogger known only by his pseudonym Jotman won the Reporters Without Borders prize in the Best of Blogs Awards 2007 for his reporting on the Saffron Revolution. Others, however, choose to set an example for other bloggers by writing under their real names despite fears of reprisal. They also argue that if the government is intent on identifying an online activist, attempts at anonymity will eventually fail. "In Saudi Arabia, there is no guarantee that you won't [be] arrested because of your frankness and speaking your mind on your blog," wrote blogger Fouad Al Farhan before he was arrested for doing just that. He still chose not to write anonymously: "But there is also no guarantee when you hide and write in Internet forums using a pseudonym."

FAME

Fame, anonymity's counterpart, is also a much-discussed way to avoid persecution. Many activists assume that public outrage will protect a famous individual from retaliation by the state. In some cases, fame can protect an activist, in other cases it can lead to problems. When the prominent Egyptian blogger Alaa Abd El-Fattah was detained in 2006 during a protest in support of an independent judiciary, an international group of activists put together the Free Alaa campaign to demand his release. After 45 days, Abd El-Fattah was indeed released. He later reported that his elevated profile had actually kept him in prison longer, since he was perceived by authorities as being a more important figure, though he also acknowledged that the fame the campaign brought protected him from being tortured. Until recently, the Cuban blogger Yoani Sánchez also used her fame to continue writing blog posts from within Cuba, but a recent abduction and beating in November of 2009 proved the limits of that strategy.

In fact, renown is often poor armor in repressive regimes. Detentions of well-known individuals, such as the Burmese comedian Zarganar or Iran's "Blogfather" Hossein Derakhshan, have clearly demonstrated that these governments have little to fear when they arrest well-known activists. In fact, these arrests send the message that the government can crack down on anybody, thus spreading fear that strengthens its power.

In more politically free countries, fame is more helpful. Governments in less politically repressive states are concerned about bad publicity and public outcry and therefore tend to back down if a great deal of attention is focused on their actions.

CAMPAIGNS

If fame and anonymity cannot save activists from being detained, can the efforts of others offer them any protection when they are imprisoned? Campaigns attempt to confer fame on an activist and, as noted in the case of Alaa Abd El-Fattah, are sometimes able to protect those who are imprisoned.

Successful campaigns include the one to free the Moroccan prankster Fouad Mourtada, imprisoned for creating a joke profile of the king's brother on Facebook, and a campaign to free the Islamist blogger Abdel Monem Mahmoud in Egypt, presumably detained for his condemnation of state-sponsored torture. Both campaigns resulted in freedom for the activist, though other factors, such as mainstream media attention and the domestic and international political climate, also played an important role.

The case of Kareem Amer, who was sentenced to four years in prison in early 2007, and which I have cited so often in this chapter, has also attracted much attention because of the Free Kareem campaign that digital activist Esra'a Al Shafei has been coordinating since Kareem's arrest. But the Free Kareem Coalition has not succeeded in securing his release nor could it prevent his being tortured.

Reliance on anonymity, fame, or campaigns to completely protect a digital activist from prisons and persecution is an insufficient strategy. Self-censorship is another option, though it implies ceasing to be an online activist. As Esra'a Al Shafei, founder of the Free Kareem Coalition, explained to me in an interview, "I do not bother discussing domestic politics [online] for the sake of my personal security, which I wish to maintain in order to continue and expand upon my work." Al Shafei, whose Mideast Youth network has launched various campaigns to support oppressed minorities in the Middle East, censors herself because she wants to continue her work on causes outside the borders of her home country. But activists who want to change their own societies cannot refrain from touching on incendiary topics. As long as no trustworthy legal system exists in their countries, they can only try not to anger the authorities and try not to become the newest casualties of political activism.

Notes

1. As with all statistics in this chapter, I acknowledge a margin of error and that other bodies collecting statistics on this topic, such as the Threatened Voices Project of Global Voices Advocacy and Reporters Without Borders, may have different figures than mine. I have made a good-faith effort to produce accurate statistics despite the efforts of many governments to obscure the truth about their political prisoners, and I apologize for any inaccuracies.

Digital Politics as Usual

Rasmus Kleis Nielsen

While we often focus on technical aspects, what is most important to keep in mind about digital activism is that it is primarily *activism*. Whether we are talking about political activism, movement activism, or issue activism, these practices are defined by individuals working in concert to achieve a common purpose. All the age-old challenges accompany such group action, no matter whether activists organize face-to-face, over the phone, or via a social networking site (increasingly, of course, they do all three). How do you get people to join? How is action coordinated? What is the common purpose? How can it be pursued? Who is your opposition and how will you confront them? No technology can answer these questions or make them go away. Instead, new tools change some of the ways in which we confront them, making some tasks easier, others harder, and leaving many unchanged.

In this chapter I will argue that we need to give up the idea that digital and networked technologies will bring about a radical break—for good or ill—with the past. Instead, we should look at how new tools and old practices are combined in modular and only sometimes innovative ways. In my view, the most important consequences of digital technologies for politics will lie neither in the creation of new futuristic kinds of "digital politics" nor in a wholesale transformation of "politics as usual," but in the integration of new tools and novel practices into what we might call the "new normal"—digital politics as usual. For example, I attended a campaign meeting as a researcher in the fall of 2007. The volunteer organizer hosting the event opened by saying, "The Internet is a great tool for people like us." I think he was right. But I am sure he was wrong when he continued, "It is because of the Internet we are all here tonight."

In the first part of this chapter, I will discuss the utility of the common idea that digital technologies have a "great potential" to totally transform politics—to make them more participatory, open, and deliberative—and explain why while this belief may in some abstract sense be true (new tools *could* do this), the notion is dangerously misleading if it is taken as a description of how digital technologies and political practices actually intersect. In the second part, I try to identify more precisely how "the Internet is a great tool" for activists, highlighting in particular the practical importance of taken-for-granted mundane tools like email, search engines, and increasingly smart phones, rather than the emerging tools (social networking sites, video sharing sites, micro-blogging sites) and specialized tools (online-integrated back-end management software and the like) that often get the most attention. In the third part, I turn to some of the problems that accompany the use of new Internet tools—mundane or not—highlighting problems of overcommunication, miscommunication, and communicative overload that political campaigns and activist groups experience as they adopt new digital technologies.

The chapter is based on data from what social scientists call ethnographic fieldwork. In 2007 and 2008, I spent hundreds of hours observing and sometimes participating in three political campaigns in the United States, one involved in a presidential primary, and two in congressional elections. The main focus of my academic research is on the mobilizing and organizing practices through which volunteers and activists are recruited and become involved in electoral politics, and the practices—digitally augmented or not—that they engage in once they become involved in the campaign. My findings may have limited applicability to other types of campaigns, but the evidence suggests that digital technologies have not brought about the end of politics as usual, nor have they been entirely subsumed under it.

These technologies are, instead, integral to the "new normal" of digital politics that increasingly relies on ubiquitous computing, always-on networks, and unequally distributed new tools and technologies, as do many other parts of our lives. What we are living through today *is* a revolution in our communications environment. But, like all other revolutions, it is best understood as the accumulation of individual acts, some continuations of existing orders, others discontinuous and innovative, all adding up to quantitative changes that lead to uneven and often only partial qualitative change. Keeping this in mind is important for those who want to understand the revolution—but perhaps even more so for the activists who want to take part in it and maybe change its course.

The Rise of "The Great Potential"

For 15 years, the "great potential" of digital technologies for activism—in electoral politics, in social movements, in civic life more generally—has been trumpeted by academics, elected officials, and political professionals. The idea of a technologically driven radical break with the past—an end to politics as usual—took off after Mosaic, the first browser, popularized the Web in 1994 and politicians and activists started to get online in greater numbers. Some saw the upset victory of the populist former wrestler Jesse Ventura in the 1998 Minnesota gubernatorial election as an example of the great potential of new technologies for political activism; his supporters had used a combination of the campaign website and various online discussion forums to organize volunteers and reach voters. Many hailed the massive protests against the World Trade Organization Ministerial Conference in 1999, the so-called Battle of Seattle, as a demonstration of the great potential of these tools for movement activism because of the rise of citizen media sites like Indymedia. Others have praised the explosive growth of MoveOn since its founding in 1998 as an illustration of the great potential digital technologies have for issue activism. Political consultant, pundit, and pontificator extraordinaire Dick Morris went one step further when he asserted, in his 1999 book, *Vote.com*, that the Internet was giving power back to the people. The big-donor-financed, television-dominated, low-turnout business-as-usual George W. Bush vs. Al Gore slugfest in the 2000 American presidential election seemed to give even the most ardent believers in the "great potential" pause—but soon enough, they were back on track, highlighting the initial success of Howard Dean's 2004 "people-powered politics," the subsequent rise of the blog-based netroots, and, in 2008, the success of the Barack Obama campaign.

The notion has its detractors, of course—one could talk about a competing narrative of "great denial," propagated by those who argue that the Internet has no discernible consequences for activism—but the idea of the "great potential" is still very much alive and well. The examples usually offered to support the great potential hypothesis have three elements in common. First, they illustrate that the idea of radical change has been with us for at least ten years (like other new information and communication technologies before it, including radio and television, the Web has inspired a lot of technological utopianism about direct democracy). Second, the examples all contain a kernel of truth in that they *do* show that Internet tools hold considerable practical promise—and represent kinds of problems that are at least somewhat novel—for various kinds of activism. Ventura *did* win, Howard Dean *did* mobilize many activists, Barack Obama *did* become president, and all three campaigns made innovative use of new technologies. Third, that very kernel of truth, however, tends to overshadow the equally important fact that the examples are all rare exceptions underlining that the great potential is rarely realized. Most gubernatorial elections are *not* won by dark-horse challengers—Internet-savvy or not. Most protests against global trade policies do *not* mobilize tens of thousands—whether they use cell phones and email or not. Most issue campaigns are *not* as successful as MoveOn, whether they are online or not. Even when they have added an "action center" to their website, most political organizations have *not* been surrounded by the kinds of activism generated around Howard Dean or Barack Obama. This is obvious within the context of American politics alone and even more so in a comparative perspective. Many countries with at least as high levels of Internet penetration and all-round technological savvy as the United States have yet to witness such spectacular examples of successful digital politics. Clearly, technology alone is not enough.

While remaining cognizant that the practical promise of new technologies is important, the incessant talk of "great potential" can be dangerously misleading if it is taken to describe the present realities of digitally augmented and Internet-assisted activism. We have no systematic evidence to suggest that the Web has given power back to the people. (Nor do I believe that any future technology will.) Those who engage in activism and politics, digital or not, need to face this squarely or they will underestimate the challenges they face—attempts at crowdsourcing that did not produce a crowd, the many instances of "flashmobbing" where no mob materialized, and the many attempts at collaborative production where no collaborators were to be found. Power is not something activists "get." It is something they build. Attempts to change the world remain uphill struggles and few take active part in them. The diffusion of ever-higher-bandwidth online access in the wealthiest parts of the world, the spread of networked mobile communications devices, and the explosive growth in the number of Internet applications that might be used for activism have not resulted in resurgent popular involvement in politics, a broader civic renaissance, or the withering away of entrenched interests or other existing powerful groups. This is, in scholar Matthew Hindman's words, "not the digital democracy we ordered."

If you find this surprising, it is because you have heard too much about the great potential and about a few exceptional cases and too little about the remaining multitude of political campaigns, social movements, and issue groups engaged in activism. Take political campaigns as an example—there are about five hundred thousand elected offices in the United States alone. Most of those running for them are not like Howard Dean, let alone Barack Obama—nor are their campaigns. While they use the Internet and their supporters often engage in digital activism, still relatively few individuals volunteer for political campaigns, despite the ever-greater use by more and more people of digital technologies for more and more tasks. In addition, remember that social movements involve only small minorities of their supposed constituencies, that issue campaigns struggle to mobilize support, and that the associational life that many consider to be central to a strong and vibrant civil society has not experienced an overall resurgence in our undoubtedly increasingly "connected age." The key value of digital activism is as poorly understood with reference to its "great potential" as it is by those in the throes of the "great denial." Its significance, instead, lies in the practical promises and problems that accompany digital politics as usual. Understanding this involves close attention to the concrete use of new tools in slow, piecemeal, and often unsatisfying, unequal, and inconclusive everyday political struggles.

From Potential to Practice: The Use of Mundane, Emerging, and Specialized Tools

Studying the actual practices of digital activists is precisely what my research focuses on. I spend much time with campaigns because I want to gather first-hand data on what staffers and volunteers actually do, in addition to what we know about what they say, what they say they do, and what other people say they do. Ethnographic fieldwork is time-consuming, sometimes inconclusive, and necessarily limited in reach, but it has the advantage of getting the researcher close to the realities of everyday life. Here, you can get a sense of what digital technologies are actually used in politics, by whom, and for what.

Even as journalists and commentators have been busy identifying recent election cycles by the year's most fashionable tool—2004 was called the "Meetup Election," 2006 the "YouTube Election," and 2008 the "Facebook Election"—close observation suggests that tools like email, search engines, and mobile phones are the ones that activists actually use the most. I refer to these as "mundane tools," a set of technologies that are widely available, almost universally used, and familiar to most. Many activists also experiment with social networking sites, video sites, and photo-sharing services—tools I refer to as "emerging" because they, while in principle available to everyone, are used only by some and are unfamiliar to many. Finally, most campaigns also use campaign websites and dedicated online-integrated software for various, more specific managerial tasks, such as managing voter databases. I call these "specialized tools" because they are not meant for general use but developed (and often sold) to handle very specific tasks and are usually known to only a few professionals.

I offer the typology of mundane, emerging, and specialized tools not because I think we can make hard-and-fast, clear-cut distinctions between them, but because I think it is useful to move beyond discussing digital activism either solely in overly specific terms of this tool or that tool or in impossibly general terms of the impact of "the Internet." People don't use "the Internet" for activism, rather they employ particular Internet tools for particular tasks. When it comes to mobilizing people to actually engage in activism, my research suggests that mundane tools are those most used.

Tools are mundane, emerging, or specialized *for someone, at some point in time, in some particular context*. The table provides an overview of how mundane and emerging tools are used today. According to surveys done by the Pew Research Center, going online is a majority preoccupation for all age groups in America under 73. But what people *do* online differs markedly from age group to age group (significant differences exist along class, race, and gender lines, too). Whereas email and search engines are almost universally adopted by all online adults, social networking sites and video sites are used much less by older people than by younger ones. YouTube and Facebook are probably entirely mundane for most readers of this book, but at the time of writing, large parts of the American (and global) population ignores them.

This is important when considering who actually gets involved in activism. Again take politics as an example. While you rarely will find a person over 30 working as a campaign staffer, many volunteers and activists are older. Data from the American National Election Studies have consistently shown not only how few people get involved in political activism (about 3 percent of the population in most recent elections, well after the Internet with its "great potential" became widely used), but also that individuals over 46 and, in particular, over 62 volunteer much more frequently than younger citizens. This distribution has important implications for the use of digital technologies to mobilize political activists. Whereas those in the younger age groups may find Facebook outreach entirely mundane, the older online generations are rarely to be found using such emerging tools and they may not stumble upon specialized tools like a campaign website and its "action center" either.

My argument is not that specialized and emerging tools do not *matter*, but that, generally speaking, mundane tools are more important when attempting to mobilize people as activists. Most campaigns, whether for political office, as part of a social movement, or as issue advocacy, involve many different actors and

	Online Teens (12–17)	Generation "Y" (18–32)	Generation "X" (33–44)	Younger Boomers (45–54)	Older Boomers (55–63)	Silent Generation (64–72)	G.I. Generation (73+)	All Online Adults
Go online	93%	87%	82%	79%	70%	56%	31%	74%
Use email	73%	94%	93%	90%	90%	91%	79%	91%
Use search engines	*	90%	93%	90%	89%	85%	70%	89%
Use social networking sites	65%	67%	36%	20%	9%	11%	4%	35%
Watch videos online	57%	72%	57%	49%	30%	24%	14%	52%

Figure 1. Adopted from Pew Internet & American Life Project (2008), "Generational Differences in Online Activities."
*No teen data for this activity.

groups, often including a more or less professionalized core of full-time staffers. Specialized tools are typically used by those at the core of a campaign to plan and manage other elements, such as volunteers and paid part-time workers (doing canvassing, etc.). Emerging tools may well be particularly important for communicating with specific constituencies for whom they are almost entirely mundane (early adopters, whether young or old). Emerging tools can also signal to the surrounding world that a certain activist group "gets it,"—that they use cutting-edge tools.

But once you move beyond issues of management and outreach to very specific target audiences, mundane tools are integral to most digital activism because they are the ones with which you can reach the widest population of potential supporters. If "build it and they will come" is the catchphrase of emerging tools and of tech entrepreneurs, activists who want to leverage the power of mundane tools should make "meet them where they are" their slogan. Email, search engines, and mobile phones are the tools staffers and activists rely on for everyday communications and coordination among one another, and these are the technologies they have in mind when they say, as one did to me, "I don't know what people did before the Internet." Activists would be fine without their campaign website or Facebook page, but would have a harder time without more ordinary Internet tools.

Such statements and the dependence they suggest may seem exaggerated, but several situations I witnessed in the course of my research suggest how deeply integrated mundane Internet tools have become to everyday campaign practices. This reliance is regularly illustrated when a particular application is not working (Gmail may be down, for example) or, more commonly, when an Internet connection fails. The latter has an effect on a campaign office akin to a kick to an anthill—staffers and volunteers start to mill around because it is no longer possible to accomplish assigned tasks. What becomes clear is that the list of people to be called was stored in Google Documents, that sending out email reminders to the weekend canvassing teams require, well, access to email—and so on. As most people who have worked or volunteered in politics know, campaign offices can function under the most appalling circumstances. The show will go on even when the toilets are clogged, the fridge resembles an improvised mold laboratory, and water seeps in through the roof, through the walls, through the floor, or through all of them. But a campaign office without an Internet connection is useless and will lie dormant until the infrastructure that underpins the tools that people rely on is made available again.

Is it banal to underline the importance of mundane tools for digital activism? I don't think so. In many other sectors, specialized or emerging tools are of much greater practical importance than mundane ones. Investment banking is arguably deeply shaped by highly specialized tools, and some parts of digital marketing seem entirely preoccupied with emerging ones. While political operatives and volunteers are certainly also often enthralled by the newest gadgets, in reality, the tools they rely on are mundane. Technologies like email, search engines, and mobile phones are not cutting-edge nor are they designed for political use. But technically, they allow for low-cost transmission, sharing, and storage of information. Socially, they connect campaigns with existing infrastructures and networked communities, allow for distributed communications among those involved, and are already familiar to users. Mundane tools like email and search engines are parts of the built communications environment that surrounds us; tools that many of those of us who live in wealthy countries are beginning to take for granted as we do running water and electricity. Even if we leave these tools behind for communication via IM or social networks and find some other way of sifting through the vast expanse of the Web, my view is that these new tools will only come to matter for political mobilization insofar as they become ordinary. When the Internet connection fails, the tools that activists miss are not the emerging or specialized ones, but the mundane ones that are integral to so much of what they do—they miss their email, not their social networking site or campaign website.

These tools don't give power back to the people or even necessarily "level the playing field." They are simply practical prostheses for collective action, making it cheaper to transmit information, easing initial group formation, making it trivial to create shared repositories of digitized knowledge. They are tools that may in the future realize the often-trumpeted "great potential," but should be understood with reference to their present practical promise and on the basis of close analysis of how they are actually used. They are important insofar as they are useful, and the less we talk about the latest gadget, the more we might appreciate the importance of mundane tools—and consider the challenges that accompany them.

Mundane Tools and Mundane Problems: Overcommunication, Miscommunication, and Communicative Overload

It would be nice to end simply by highlighting how email and the like can help activists change the world, but close attention to how people use digital technologies in politics suggest that there is another side to the story about how they are used. Mundane tools based on new digital technologies come hand-in-hand with widespread and equally mundane problems of "too much information." Ironically, it is precisely because these tools allow for such low-cost data transmission, group formation, and conversation that they are accompanied by an increasingly pronounced set of interrelated problems involving overcommunication and miscommunication on the part of organizers who send messages and communicative overload on the part of volunteers who receive them. The costs of transmitting and storing information have declined dramatically, but the human cost of processing information has not changed substantially. In 15 years, we have gone from a situation in which the cost of communication was a central obstacle for activists to one in which its very cheapness and abundance present new and different challenges. Communication is good, sure—but you can have too much of a good thing.

A widely shared belief among staffers and veteran campaign volunteers is that "you can't repeat things too often." As long as each repetition took time and effort for the person communicating something, this was probably true. But today, campaigns frequently appear to repeat things too often, leading to overcommunication. Observation and conversations with activists suggest that people receive the same information over and over again, as the same messages are delivered repeatedly by email (often several times, some forwarded, and posted on multiple listservs), via social networking sites, via feeds from websites, and often via phone, too. At some point (and it no doubt differs from person to person and group to group), what may have started as useful reminders becomes redundant information. One common reaction to the problem of overcommunication is voiced by a volunteer who, when asked about how he dealt with all the email he got from the organizers told me, "I just ignore it, man." Instead, he explained that he relied on cues from select other members of the group he was part of, trusting that "my friends will let me know if there is something I need to know."

A more serious problem is miscommunication, discrepancies between different discrete messages among activists (or between staffers and volunteers). To quote from one of the emails I received in the course of my fieldwork: "Oops, I made a mistake. Here it is again." Obviously, mistakes have always and will always be made when people communicate, in activist groups or elsewhere. One side of the problem of miscommunication is a variation of the problem of overcommunication but further complicated by the need to make choices between conflicting messages. The problem of miscommunication is also compounded by the ever-increasing number of platforms used to communicate. It is one thing to ensure a minimum of miscommunication when trying to maintain the consistency of emails. But avoiding misinformation becomes more difficult when keeping track of content on numerous platforms, from the campaign website, to Meetup, Facebook, and so on. Information is particularly susceptible to miscommunication when details are changed at the last minute. Does the meeting start at 6 p.m. or 8 p.m.? Is it at venue A or venue B? Should one trust the email sent out yesterday, the details on the MySpace page, or the post on the campaign website? Again, activists experiencing this problem have to develop their own methods of coping and will sometimes lose touch with the campaign.

Of course, in many cases, those at the receiving end chose not to deal with overcommunication and miscommunication—leading to the problem of communicative overload, whether understood as a decision not to deal with too much information or the lack of capacity to do so. The costs of sorting relevant from irrelevant information are shifting from sender to receiver *because* sending messages has become so easy, with so many ways of sending (email, IM, social networking sites, text messaging, in addition to posting it on various websites and social networking sites, blogs, and micro-blogging sites), and because the transmission costs are so low, the sender can with little effort send a message again (or post it again). Another activist I interviewed was incredulous when I asked her about the steady stream of emails from the organizers and asked me, "You mean to say you read all of that s—?" Of course, she was right to be surprised. Arguably, many people did not. This is precisely what is significant here, that cheap communications have led to a situation where the receivers have to deal with abundant amounts of material and make their own choices—choices that only in the most fortuitous of circumstances will lead them to read what the organizers, if pressed to prioritize, would have considered to be the most important.

The problem is, however, that *they too* are often overloaded, especially if they are at the center of a traditional hub-and-spoke form of organizing, where most information has to go through them. As one organizer confided, "I don't know what to do with all of this."

The supreme irony here is that the solution to problems of overcommunication, miscommunication, and communicative overload is often more communication—"I'll send it again." (To quote another email.) Thus, in about fifteen years, communication among activists and with potential activists has gone from being an (analog) bottleneck to a (digital) fire hose, the challenges of getting the word out have evolved into the new challenge of getting the right amount of words to the right people at the right time. Problems of "too much information" may have been reserved for an elite few in top positions in the past, but seem to be increasingly widespread and broad-based. So focus shifts to timely, relevant, and actionable information. Many activist groups have—like most government entities and corporations—been faster at adopting new digital technologies than at adapting to them. This is not a critique of the people involved, and it should be accompanied by the observation that people are increasingly searching for ways to manage the problems of overcommunication, miscommunication, and communicative overload briefly discussed here. In some cases, short-term solutions are sought, and they often take the form of a fallback on earlier forms of organizing, where standard operating procedures, hierarchies and authority, or informal on- and/or offline networks of trust and reputation help people sort and manage information. This was the standard reaction in the three campaigns I researched; elsewhere, however, we can observe more encouraging attempts to use new technologies in more innovative ways—collaborative filtering, recommendation systems, and new forms of organizing. Such new practices and technological filters allow groups to increase the overall amount of communication without being paralyzed by overcommunication, miscommunication, and communicative overload.

Conclusion

The new technologies that help and hinder activists are already integral to the "new normal" of highly wired, digitally augmented, and Internet-assisted political campaigns. Mundane tools like email, search engines, and mobile phones are central to how activists communicate and organize today, even as they also present new problems of overcommunication, miscommunication, and communicative overload. Generalizations as to whether the net benefit is positive or negative are hard to make and probably not useful—since new technologies are increasingly ubiquitous and here to stay, rejecting them even if they are deemed impractical would mean a self-imposed exile from the shared built communications environment. These tools are part of how we *live* now and will be part of how we *act*. The pursuit of their practical promise requires neither paeans of praise to the "great potential" nor the solemn sermons of the "great denial," but ongoing experimentation, information sharing, and development of best practices aimed at making new technologies useful for those who face the old and new challenges that accompany activism in the digital politics as usual.

The Future of Advocacy in a Networked Age

Sem Devillart and Brian Waniewski

Digital technologies are driving many of the changes involving activists, advocacy groups, and other nongovernmental organizations today. These technologies have given more people more access to information, as well as to the tools of production, communication, and distribution than ever before. Such access and the communication technologies that enable it have weakened long-standing hierarchies of power and access and lowered the barriers to entry and success in just about every industry and endeavor. Partially as a result, the number of individuals and groups participating in civil society has increased dramatically in the last few decades. According to the Union of International Associations, the number of international nongovernmental organizations alone grew some 700 percent between 1980 and 2007. More groups have resulted in more pressure to innovate and differentiate. What has also become more important is communicating vision, mission, values, and results cleverly, coherently, and quickly across old and new media. Such fragmentation may be only the leading edge of the changes we can expect digital technologies to drive in coming decades. Soon, we may not even be discussing "digital advocacy" or "digital activism," ancient activities dressed up in new methods by high-tech tools. Instead, the activities of civic development may have evolved into forms qualitatively different from the "advocacy" and "activism" of today, forms based on the logic of the networks that our digital devices depend on.

We are leaving the era of print and entering the digital age. Nowadays texts, sounds, images, and other information are instantly transmitted over networks. By examining the logic and structure of these networks, then imagining analogous ways of thinking or doing that might emerge in the future, we may be able to gain insight into how advocacy and activism will evolve. The forms advocacy and activism may take in the future will address the changes, problems, and pressures of today, since these pressures arise out of a disharmony between old methods and modes of thinking and the new reality arising. So, let us begin with a look at a few of the problems currently bedeviling activists, advocacy groups, and other nongovernmental organizations. Then we will explore how more "networked" forms of advocacy or activism might help address them.

Activism in an Information-Rich Environment: Overload, Interconnection, and the Sense-Making Power of the Network

Today, because of the Internet, we enjoy access to more information on people, places, and events than ever before. No matter how specialized our interests, chances are we can indulge them. And, if we cannot, we have everything we need to create a new "channel," making available to everyone on Earth the fruits of our pet fascinations. In real time, we can follow the daily routines of endangered Amazonian lizards. Or we can witness the murder of indigenous leaders as they oppose the machinery used to mine tribal lands. Moreover, in an instant, we can pull up a map of the disputed territory or delve into the minutiae of modern strip mining. We can browse world commodity markets for the latest copper futures data or skim the translated remarks of indignant political officials. The kind of research that, even a decade ago, would have taken days and dedicated detective work is now available in minutes to every moderately curious, Internet-savvy Dick and Jane.

The vast information buffet at our fingertips is not without disadvantages, however. One commonly discussed disadvantage is that authority or accuracy is no longer a given. With a little design sophistication, any opinion can be made to look like the well-considered output of disinterested experts. Even the appearance of scientific consensus can be manufactured. Thus, confusion and disinformation are easily introduced at a very early stage in issues-based advocacy. As the debate over climate change has revealed, the public's interest in an issue can be exhausted in disputes of basic fact, rather than in the identification or analysis of the problem or possible solutions.

Another related, frequently discussed disadvantage of our information-rich environment is that we tend to be aware of and understand a much broader array of issues much less deeply. This is the result of the volume of information available to us every day and the finite amount of time we have to assimilate it. Such shallow understanding is also connected with the formats of Internet-based information. These tend toward brief texts, captioned images, and video clips, which continue to shrink in length, area, and/or duration as we look to mobile devices to inform us on the go. Thus, organizations working to move and inform minds around issues both complex and subtle, for example, the reform of the U.S. health-care system, often are at a deep disadvantage when trying get their entire message heard.

Even more problematic and fundamental is the fact that, although our knowledge has become more generally broad, we tend to lack the perspective required to navigate murky waters with calm. Why? Because online information has been presented in terms very similar to the information in printed texts, with one important difference. In printed texts, information is embedded in a connective tissue of overlapping arguments or threads of reasoning. Some threads are short, spanning a sentence or a paragraph, and some consume a whole article, chapter, book, or subject area. These threads give readers a sense of how all the various bits of information interconnect. Together, they form a clear point of view, in relationship to which readers can locate themselves and "take a stand." The same is true online, within the less rigorous context of Web posts, pages, and sites. The hyperlink offers users liberation from the connective tissue of any one argument, point of view, page, or frame. Users can leap between linked bits of information at will and without end, never developing a sense of how the bits fit together, a sense of perspective, or interconnection. Without this sense, many find it difficult to develop a stable relationship to the information taken in or to connect it in meaningful, memorable ways to lived experience. So, for example, while we may know more about the living conditions of poor Honduran farmers, we may have trouble seeing how their plight affects our daily lives as the consumers of the agricultural products they produce.

Strange that the Internet—a system of interconnected networks—may diminish the sense of interconnection we feel. But the fact is, with less than a quarter century of general use, the Internet's resources have been focused mainly on connecting people to information, organizations, things, places, and other people, rather than on interconnecting ideas or concepts in systems to help us make sense of ourselves and the world we live in. The Internet has tended to act as an endlessly expandable, low-cost encyclopedia, newspaper, magazine, movie theater, catalogue, brochure, book, bulletin board, phone directory, etc., rather than as the most powerful sense-making tool yet created.

The shift toward sense-making will occur when organizations find a clear, visually compelling way to display and allow users to interact with the rich interconnections that underlie reality but that may not be immediately evident. Once such means are in place, users will be able to see at a glance, for instance, the global ramifications of the hamburger they ate at their favorite fast food place. They will be able to track inputs and outputs throughout production and distribution processes and learn how these affect rural communities, farming practices, health care, food safety, and international trade relations. They will be able to delve into each ramification for more detail and depth, all the while cognizant of the path followed and how the ramifications relate to one another, as well as to the hamburger that set in motion the chain reaction of interconnected consequences. Organizations will be able to move beyond trying to convince individuals why they should care about food politics and related issues and instead offer them a system through which to explore for themselves the many ways these issues touch and fundamentally construct their lives. This shift will be akin to helping a traveler from point A to point B with a satellite image of the location, rather than with verbal or written directions. The traveler can thereby grasp all the many features of the locality she must navigate and how they relate to one another, then choose for herself the best route. She can abstract herself from her on-the-ground reality in order to envision a bigger picture, her place therein, and how movement on her part might alter the situation she and others face.

A sense of overview and interconnection has always been a critical prerequisite to the work of advocates, activists, and other awareness-raising groups. These are the first steps toward moving hearts and minds and inspiring meaningful action. But until the network that lies at the heart of reality, and that nature reflects, is made explicit—along with the interconnections that naturally lead to concern and even love—advocacy groups will struggle to convince a public unable to connect information out-there to reality in-here why anything matters.

Beyond Us vs. Them: From Contradiction to Compassion

Activists and advocacy groups have typically been repositories of values or points of view considered challenging to the status quo. This built-in sense of opposition contributes to an "us vs. them" mentality. Most organizations have abandoned the radical techniques of early activism in favor of the more businesslike methods of marketing and media relations or practices like culture-jamming, in which mainstream cultural institutions or their symbols are parodied or otherwise disrupted. But every now and then, young angry voices hammer the face shields of riot cops and rubber bullets fly. Even putting such real-world radicalism aside, great quantities of money, energy, and intelligence are poured into the pro-con, right-wrong, left-right, good-evil rhetorical flurries that define network news programming and the tone of public debate off and online.

It is tempting for organizations to adopt competitive strategies toward peers engaged in like or complementary efforts, and the pressure to secure funding is especially acute in today's financial climate. Thus, to impugn the methods or mettle of "competing" organizations can seem like the easiest path to success, a path well worn by the commercial sector.

A culture of us vs. them prevails even among advocacy organizations that share common goals and common opponents. Such attitudes can sometimes be observed, for example, among the more than one thousand groups that compete for federal cancer funding in the United States. The American Cancer Society, concerned that competition might diminish the effectiveness of efforts to eliminate cancer, has sought to organize "competitors" into coalitions such as One Voice Against Cancer. More recent cancer coalitions, like C-Change, cast an even broader net by bringing together drug and media companies, universities, hospitals, insurers, grant-making institutions, and government bodies:

all the players one would expect with a stake in the research, treatment, or elimination of cancer. What about organizations with a financial stake in maintaining the economic incentives and behavioral choices that are conducive to cancer—companies that pollute our air and drinking water and market carcinogenic products? A coalition that does not include or work to transform such organizations will never succeed in eliminating cancer. At best, it may successfully address specific kinds or clusters of cancer.

Forming coalitions may create economies of scale and the possibility of broader reach, but coalitions will never succeed in addressing the challenges that threaten our future as a species. Such challenges seem complex, systematic, and unaddressable precisely because we face in them the deep ambivalence at the core of our culture and being. We are at war with ourselves; our institutions are at war with one another. One arm creates a problem that the other arm scrambles to fix. We want to lower our carbon emissions, for instance, but fear losing the high profits and abundance of cheap products we treasure. To face this conflict in ourselves is extremely painful. We prefer to externalize it in an enemy, to manufacture disputes, to choose sides, to prefer "this" to the exclusion or demonization of "that." In doing so, we are doomed never to be free of the enemies we create, the problems we face, and the labor of managing the consequences.

To free ourselves from these problems more effectively, we must find some way to move beyond "us vs. them" and rectify the contradictions—internal and external—that underlie it. We have already touched on how the structure of the Internet compresses the distance between potentially divergent points of view. With a mouse click, we can jump from the site of an organization like Greenpeace to the site of Dow Chemical and find points of view forged not in the reactive heat of debate but in the relative peace of collectively held strong convictions. We can experience the full force of the contradictions they establish. To experience deep contradictions in the information we take in has never been easy, and the decentralized structure of the Internet does not help matters. On the Internet, everything is information, and, from a system's perspective, all existing information is equally valid and true. No centralized or organizing order, no Dewey decimal system, or trusted curator keeps subject areas or sympathies separate. While some users may be confused, others may find they have a new recognition of and comfort with the contradictions basic to human beings and the world we construct to live in. The ability to act effectively while honoring and holding contradictions in mind may become more widespread. More people may come to understand and behave as if the deeds of Greenpeace and Dow Chemical are both equally the collective results of men and women facing their circumstances to the best of their abilities.

To honor contradiction is a first step toward compassion.

In the future, organizations may move beyond the advocacy of single points of view, evolving into vehicles for compassion and spaces where people can examine all the points of view in a culture in relation to particular issues—where they can explore and reflect on the real-world ramifications of these points of view, engage in respectful discussion, and perhaps discover some higher common purpose into which contradictory impulses, like the impulse to conserve the planet and the impulse to mine at all costs its resources, can be integrated. This would mark a significant transition from advocacy as a zero-sum game to advocacy as collaborative problem-solving across interests.

Opening Up Advocacy: From Internally-Focused Institutions to Networked Systems

As we move toward systems that make explicit the interconnection of all creation and as we come to accept the contradictions interconnection establishes, new forms of collective action may arise that will be less institution-bound, more spontaneous, and better coordinated. These forms of action will rest on a shared awareness of those places, problems, or causes wherein, by applying the least collective effort, maximum change can result. Just as an acupuncturist stimulates points on and just below the skin to produce deep systemic healing, we may begin to locate and act on those areas of the social body where a little extra attention can bring about the transformation of challenges in disparate sectors.

Currently, coordinating action among groups is difficult. We all agree it is necessary. We all agree that no one approach or organization working in isolation can successfully address global challenges like climate change or poverty. Yet, again and again, in our attempts to coordinate, we founder. This may be because activists tend to focus on whatever world region, approach, problem, tool, demographic, or combination thereof has come to define them as institutions. Foundational stories can often be located in these points of focus; an institution's identity and worldview tend to take shape and harden around these points of focus. Institutional attachments and interests can be established that are so strong that an organization can neither examine very candidly the world's changing needs nor evaluate how well these are being addressed by "business-as-usual."

Focus is a constructive attribute to bring to any task, and it is necessary to the effective operation of any institution. But focus applied too soon, too rigorously, or too much as a matter of course can hamper the ability to assess a complex situation deeply, conceive creative responses, and act with grace and spontaneity. It is precisely these faculties that groups must bring to the table to combine their collective strengths, identify collaborative solutions, and coordinate implementation.

A common way of freeing these faculties among institutional groups is through a strategic alliance, task force, or other umbrella-like body. If the convening purpose of the body is sufficiently strong, individuals may surrender the focus of the institutions they represent and begin to see with new eyes the world and its challenges. If its purpose is too partisan, however, excessive formalization becomes a temptation, and members may end up with an organization whose points of view and processes are every bit as ossified as the institutions they came together to escape. If the animating purpose is too weak, the body may devolve into a venue for back-patters, blabbers, and bullies. No one will feel moved to step beyond habitual positions and fully engage.

To build and maintain a strategic alliance is a delicate task, but to use that alliance as a platform for groups to collaborate and coordinate action effectively is downright heroic. Perhaps another way is possible. Let us begin by assuming that organizations have found a clear, compelling means to display the rich interconnections that underlie reality, as discussed above. For example, an organization concerned with industrial farming practices has found a way to map how these practices affect everything from individual and community health at home to economic development abroad, the migration patterns of refugee and immigrant populations, international security, and so on. This map of interconnected information will be a useful "sales tool" in discussions with donors, strategic allies, corporate partners, and government advocates because it will help listeners visualize how seemingly distant issues, causes, or problems fundamentally construct their reality.

These maps have an even greater potential. As more and more organizations come to build them around their issues, the data they contain could be aggregated, compared, and evaluated to determine, for instance, which ramifications or factors recur most frequently in particular geographies or across the globe. In this way, a number of groups concerned with malaria, poverty alleviation, HIV-AIDS, and the spread of genetically modified crops in Africa, for example, could come together, perform a comparison, and discover that the strongest factor their issues share is the health of women in rural communities. These groups would then have a more objective basis for the identification of common goals, and these goals might better guide collective decision making. As a result, these groups might choose to pool their resources to remove a problem previously viewed as secondary to their primary focus. The removal of that "secondary" problem could occasion broader systemic improvements that serve to alleviate "primary" problems, just as an acupuncturist, applying attention to one area of the body, effects healing throughout.

Taken together and interconnected in networks, such maps could become powerful tools to help visualize humankind's vast social body and give the groups dedicated to its improvement a means of identifying the most pressing common points of interest. This, in turn, could lead to more objective diagnoses of the challenges we face as a species, as well as a more intelligent allocation of resources, more effective coordination, and more targeted treatment.

Such a network of maps could also lead to forms of action both highly distributed and coordinated, if nongovernmental organizations combine their potential with the connecting, facilitating powers of the Web. If today's organizations tend to be highly focused, structured, and staffed issues-based centers of action turned outward to gather resources, deliver goods and services, and spread the word, in the future, they could become more light and nimble, offering open interconnected frameworks for people to organize spontaneously and act as needed. The organizations of the future could be more like R&D labs or thought leaders, offering the overview, tools, infrastructure, and incentives needed to inspire innovative, self-directed, local response. Collaboratively, they could build shared awareness of those common causes or problems where attention is most needed to heal the world's body. Then, they could offer the resources people need to respond.

We are especially enthusiastic about the potential for such maps and look forward to opportunities and collaborations that allow us to further develop them and move closer to their realization.

We are also very heartened by the potential for new forms of activism and advocacy in the digital age. At their best and at their core, these forms of social development embody and express the network's primary structural characteristic: connection. Compare this to the principles of division that all too often underlie the commercial interests that bring us today's technological splendors, and it is easy to see that the age to come belongs to social developers and those who strive to do good, no matter the form it takes.

Conclusion: Building the Future of Digital Activism

Mary Joyce

Digital Activism Decoded has mapped the past and present of digital activism. How can we now build its future? The field's ultimate success or failure will be determined by the daily practice of digital activists. For digital activists to succeed in using digital tools in contests against the forces of oppression and injustice, those practices must continually increase in effectiveness. Thus, the success of digital activism lies in creating sustainable means for the continual improvement of practice.

The Dilemma of Tactical Knowledge

Currently, digital activism advances by creating and disseminating best practices in tactical knowledge—lessons on how to use a specific digital tool in a given context to achieve a strategic goal. Advisers in this field, Ivan Boothe and Rachel Happe among them, provide recommendations of this kind to nonprofits and advocates, while training organizations like Tactical Technology Collective produce guides and, recently, a film: *10 Tactics*. DigiActive, an organization I cofounded, also creates posts about tactical best practices from around the world and guides to using specific social media applications for activism.

Tactical knowledge, while extremely important to improving activism practice, has its shortcomings. Each tactic is highly contextual: a given practice, using a specific tool, was successful in achieving a given goal by targeting a given audience within an equally specific political, economic, and social context. Reproducing tactics is common, yet blueprint copying is impossible. Even in the same country, the context always changes from campaign to campaign. The April 6 strike in Egypt was a successful online mobilization in 2008; a year later, the same tactics used to mobilize on the same date failed to produce widespread participation.

This leaves the disseminators of tactical knowledge with two options: specificity and generalization. The strength of specificity—of disseminating the exact details of a successful campaign, as DigiActive does—is that knowledge about the latest innovations and tools is conveyed to a wider audience. Its weakness arises from the field's quickly changing best practices; accordingly specific tactics have a short shelf life. E-petitions were effective lobbying tools in the United States at the end of the twentieth century. Overutilization and revelations about the ease of participation have greatly lessened the impact of such activism. Facebook and Twitter are now very popular activism tools. They are almost certain to become less effective; if they do remain of significant value to activists, the successful practices associated with them will certainly have changed.

The second option is generalization, extrapolating more widely applicable but less tool-specific lessons from a variety of cases. This is the methodology of Tactical Technology Collective's film, in which the 10 tactics—like "mobilize people," "witness and record," and "use collective intelligence"—do not rely on specific software applications or devices for their implementation or validity. The film takes a hybrid approach—pairing these general lessons with specific examples. Contemporary examples, however, may become dated in just a few months even if the general lessons are still valid, making the training material lose its appeal to activists.

This dilemma of tactical knowledge creates a catch-22 for advocates who wish to disseminate the best practices of digital activism. Should they discuss how to use specific tools based on recent successful cases? They may then see the best practice lose relevance in a few months as tools and contexts change. Or should they disseminate general best practices that leave activists to fill in the blanks about what tools to use and in which context the best practice can be implemented successfully? Both of these options have serious shortcomings. Is there a better way to make digital activists more effective?

The Strategic Knowledge Gap

Despite the shortcomings of tactical knowledge, the field of digital activism relies on it because activists do not yet have their own body of strategic knowledge—a set of analytical tools that can be used across a wide range of contexts. The best we can do now—and what the best purveyors of tactical knowledge rely on—is to take bodies of strategic knowledge from the pre-digital era and apply them to the new field of digital activism. What areas should be mined for their insights and tactics? Public relations has useful advice about strategic communications, cause branding, and message dissemination. Earlier activists created strategies of community organizing, including the use of supporter social networks for recruitment, power mapping of allies and opponents, and leadership through devolution of authority to local organizers. The field of nonviolent civil resistance also provides a body of knowledge about how authoritarian regimes are sustained and how they can be destabilized. Scholars of media and communications call upon ideas like information cascades to describe how peripheral knowledge can pervade a society, changing the perceptions and realities of political power.

All these bodies of knowledge have a place for digital technology and illuminate the field, yet they cannot be directly applied to the digital world. Developed in a pre-digital era, they conceptualize media and communication in a pre-digital way: peer-to-peer networked behavior is only possible at the local level, while mass communication takes place through broadcast. This was true in the era of television, radio, newspapers, and landline phones; it is no longer true in the digital era of the global network. The infrastructure of activism has changed, yet our strategic knowledge has not.

How important is this gap in strategic knowledge? Some maintain that digital activism does not need its own strategic knowledge because it is, in fact, merely an extension of existing practices—a change of degree but not of kind. However, if the radical change in how people communicate is, indeed, a game changer, the lack of strategic knowledge could be limiting. Without a framework with which to understand their potential actions, digital activists resort to blueprint copying and guess-and-check. Many activists simply recreate pre-digital forms of activism using digital tools: the protest march is organized by social network instead of clandestine meetings, the mass mailing becomes a mass email. Because deep understanding of the potential of digital infrastructure for activism is lacking, so is sophistication and successful implementation. Sometimes activists succeed in their digital campaigns; sometimes the powerful governments, corporations, and interest groups that are their opponents win. Current practice has certainly not convinced the skeptics of digital activism's value. With better understanding, we can change our strategies and make digital activists more effective in their practice and, thus, help the potential of digital activism to become a reality.

Building Strategic Knowledge for the Field of Digital Activism

In the Preface, we talked about the lack of "foundational knowledge," the need to understand "underlying mechanics," to create "frameworks." Of all the types of foundational knowledge that could be useful to the field of digital activism, strategic knowledge is the most valuable in improving digital activism practice.

How can this strategic knowledge be encouraged? It is too big a job for one scholar, one institution, one grand project. It must be crowd-sourced, with the best practitioners, scholars, researchers, and thinkers encouraged to engage in the effort. Rigorous analysis and comparability of claims must be undertaken. Currently, a variety of claims about digital activism can be made and case studies cherry-picked to back up assertions. Because case studies are highly contextual, they afford little basis for comparability and gauging the relative validity of a given case study can be difficult.

In the Introduction, it was suggested that foundational knowledge could be created by applying rigorous and comparable quantitative analysis to the qualitative assertions of case studies. While true, it is only part of the story. More than any type of research or analysis, the field of digital activism needs the human and informational infrastructure with which strategic knowledge can be created and on which it can be based. Human infrastructure entails a network connecting the key thought leaders in the field to one another and to practitioners. Representatives from nonprofit, for-profit, government, and academic institutions would need to be included.

Informational infrastructure would also need to be created to allow such thought leaders and practitioners to speak to one another without shared interests being lost in translation. In addition, a common terminology would be needed so that, for example, the proponent of liberation theology and the proponent of online organizing can more easily discover areas of shared interest. A common agenda for the creation of strategic knowledge would also be needed. For academics, a common set of data-coding standards would allow for greater comparability of research and make spotting trends easier. For governments, who seek to help digital activists around the world in order to achieve foreign policy goals, a clear framework within which to judge the likelihood of digital activism success would help them focus their energy on key structural factors that are impeding activism's effectiveness. For-profit companies, such as device makers, might be convinced to design their tools in a way that does not endanger activists or compromise their privacy. An ambitious and complex project, yes—but a possible one.

Imagining the Future

Perhaps the greatest motivator for this kind of collaborative creation would be a shared vision of what is possible if the great potential of digital activism is realized—of the potentially transformative power of ubiquitous and dense linkages between citizens across the world. A new power grid is available and it is us. Unlike a traditional electrical power grid—a network in which power is generated only at the central point of production and money flows into the center while electricity flows out—this new human power grid would have many points of generation and almost infinite interfaces.

The new power grid is a decentralized network of individuals, each of whom can both produce and consume information, interact with the media, take action, and engage in protest. At the edges of the network, the term "consumer" does not apply anymore. While the organizer of an action may be called a "producer," supporters who participate in the action are producers as well. The action *is* its participants.

The infrastructure of this new grid is the cables and radio signals that make up increasingly interconnected Internet and phone networks. The infrastructure is composed of applications like SMS and social networks that allow us to connect to one another with astonishing speed, increasing ease, and greater complexity. What will we do with this new network of software and infrastructure that connects us? What will happen when the power of the individual is organized through the grid and begins to push back on the center, the traditional locus of authority? How will the center change? Or will it not change at all?

Central authority, in the form of both governments and corporations, has always functioned through the cooperation of individuals within those institutions. The institution gets its power from the reliability of cooperation among the individuals within the institution. This reliability of cooperation used to require intense capital investment—the payment of salaries to soldiers or bureaucrats.

Traditional institutions are resource-intensive because they are forced to use extrinsic motivators like fear and money to ensure a significant and reliable level of cooperation. Digital campaigns, in contrast, can achieve their cooperation goals with radically fewer financial resources because a permanent time commitment is not necessary and a cause appeals to the idealism of the supporter, a free and intrinsic motivation. If many people can be engaged at low time commitment and low cost instead of high time commitment and high cost, as Harvard professor Yochai Benkler has posited in his book *The Wealth of Networks*, new institutions will arise.

Today, free and ad hoc organizations have demonstrated their ability to cooperate on discrete projects—a worldwide day of action, for instance—but have rarely formed the durable institutions that make cooperation reliable and would give them real power. This is one reason why it is so important that strategic knowledge be created. Digital activism needs to improve. Today we see marches, tomorrow we may see alternative political structures.

Field-building and facilitating alternative political structures seem impossibly difficult. What can we, as activists or potential activists, do to shape the future of digital activism?

I'd like to answer those questions with a story from a close friend who is a professional futurist. At first, I was quite skeptical of her vocation. "Isn't it impossible to predict the future?" I asked.

"Well," she responded, "I don't predict the future, I help my clients build it."

"What do you mean?" I prodded.

"Well, let's say that a futurist determines that in five years, blue is likely be popular. That futurist is employed by a multinational corporation, the kind of organization that can afford to hire a futurist in the first place."

"Go on," I said, intrigued.

"That corporation starts designing, and then manufacturing, products that are blue: cars, toaster ovens, T-shirts, nail polish. Pretty soon, you do start seeing a lot more blue around. But the future didn't just happen, it was created."

In this digital world, where the individual has more capacity to learn, communicate, and collaborate than ever before, we also have the ability to create the future of digital activism. It is our future to build, our world to change.

Glossary

compiled by Talia Whyte and Mary Joyce

astroturf: The appearance of a grassroots campaign that is, in fact, organized by an established institution. This controversial practice is commonly used to benefit specific individuals or groups who have funded the campaign. In the world of digital activism, astroturfing can take the form of paid blogging or other supposedly spontaneous and personal communication that is actually determined by payments from an interest group.

autofollow: To automatically subscribe to another user's feed (content stream) on the micro-blogging site Twitter. This indiscriminate practice is generally frowned upon as it implies that the user is not reviewing another user's content before deciding to subscribe. Autofollowing is also used as a means of increasing a user's followers. A user may follow multiple users at random in the hope that they will reciprocate with an autofollow.

blog (or Weblog): A regularly updated online journal, with the most recent entry at the top of the page. Written either by an individual or a group of writers in a conversational manner, blog posts most often contain links, audio, video, and other information found online juxtaposed with the blogger's viewpoint on that content. Most blogs allow readers to post comments about what is being discussed on the blog.

blogroll: A list of recommended blogs, displayed as a series of links, on a blog's sidebar

blogware (or Weblog software): Support software for blogs. Such software allows users to both write and share content. Products such as Blogger, Wordpress, and Typepad are examples of blogware.

bot: A piece of software that carries out automated actions, often malicious, directed against another computer system.

bot attack: A destructive or disruptive assault on a computer system carried out by a network of computers running bots.

botnet: A combination of "robot" and "network," a botnet is a network of automated software controlled and manipulated by a third party, that is, neither the owner of the machine running the bot nor the target of the attack. A botnet can refer to a legitimate group of computers that share program processing. However, the term generally refers to computers running malicious software that was downloaded without the consent of the computer's owner and is used to make attacks against other systems.

clickthrough rate (CTR): A measure of the success of an online advertising or advocacy campaign. The CTR measures what percentage of the people who viewed a piece of online promotional content clicked on that content to arrive at the destination site.

crowdsourcing: A distributed labor practice wherein a job that is usually done by one person is given to a large group of people who each do a smaller piece of the task, usually as volunteers. In digital activism, a group of supporters may donate a wide variety of content and skills (video, photos, Web design, etc.) to a cause, thus allowing a dynamic campaign to emerge with limited expenditure of financial resources.

cyber-activism: Campaigning and organizing for political and social change in cyberspace, an alternative virtual world composed of interactive online communities and immersive experiences. This 1990s view of Internet activism—that it occurs in an online space that is separate from the real world—has lost favor as activists and organizers have increasingly stressed the importance of online action having offline impact.

data trail: A record of information about a person's actions that remains after the action is complete and that can be accessed by others and used to track that person's activities, often without the individual's knowledge or consent. The Internet makes the collection and retention of data—and the leaving of data trails—easier than it was in the paper era.

digital activism: The practice of using digital technology to increase the effectiveness of a social or political change campaign.

distributed denial of service (DDoS): An explicit attempt by Internet attackers to prevent legitimate users from accessing a website or other online service. Attackers make repeated requests to the website, sometimes by simply reloading a Web page in their browsers or, more often, by using a botnet or other software to create automatic requests. The high number of requests overloads the capacity of the servers on which the site is housed, thus the servers are no longer capable of responding to requests—either legitimate or illegitimate—from people trying to access the site, often resulting in the display of an error message to the site's visitors.

e-activism: The use of electronic tools to increase the effectiveness of a social or political change campaign. In the early days of computing, the "e" preface was useful in differentiating between activities that were and were not mediated by a computer, for example email and e-banking. Since the rise of the Internet, the electronic nature of computing is seen as less salient than its networking features and the "e" prefix is, as a result, less popular than it once was.

e-advocacy: The use of electronic tools for political and social change in cases in which the campaigners are speaking (advocating) on behalf of a particular group or interest.

flaming: The act of posting deliberately hostile messages online, generally in chat rooms and on discussion boards. While most "flamewars" start out as a heated debate over a political or social issue, some malicious Internet users (trolls) flame for the sole purpose of offending other users.

flashmob: A large group of people who gather suddenly in public to engage in unusual and concerted actions and then disperse quickly. Part of the larger smart mob phenomenon, these gatherings are usually organized through social media, text messaging, or email, and have a grassroots character that differentiates them from publicity stunts with a profit motive.

follow: In an online context, to subscribe to a user's content stream (feed) on the micro-blogging site Twitter.

hashtag: Community-driven tagging convention mostly used on the micro-blogging site Twitter to aggregate and track content by subject, with the use of a hash symbol (#) followed by a key word, or tag. An example is #4change, a hashtag for tweets on the use of social media for social change.

Hype Cycle: A visualization, developed by the American research firm Gartner, that shows the life of certain technologies. The five phases of a Hype Cycle are technology trigger, peak of inflated expectations, trough of disillusionment, slope of enlightenment, and plateau of productivity.

info-activism: The use of effective information and communications practices to enhance advocacy work, of which digital technology is only one possible medium. The term is most commonly associated with the advocacy training organization Tactical Technology Collective.

malware: Malicious software designed to enter a computer owner's system without his or her consent and to execute destructive or disruptive functions. Once installed on a user's system, the software carries out malicious actions (unintended by the system's owner) that affect the system of the user or a third-party target.

mashup: An application that contains two or more sources of digitally encoded information in formats such as video, audio, text, or graphics; this juxtaposition highlights in new ways how the pieces of information are related. A popular example of a mashup is the crisis-mapping software Ushahidi, which allows users to view mobile text messages superimposed on a digital map according to the message's place of origin.

meme: In an online context, a piece of content that spreads widely on the Internet without changing its basic structure. The content of the meme can be an inside joke, an image, or a response to a prompt such as the creation of a "top five" list on a given topic.

memetic entropy: Chaos in the transmission of a piece of structurally-stable content, a meme, as it is shared from person to person online.

micro-blog: A form of blogging (a personal Weblog or online diary) that allows users to broadcast short messages to subscribers. Twitter is currently the most popular micro-blogging service.

nano-activism: A play on the prefix "nano," which means $\frac{1}{10^9}$ in size, this term refers to an activism methodology that breaks the work of the campaign into small and easily executable tasks by using technology in innovative ways, such as signing online petitions, joining special interest groups on Facebook, or many people donating small amounts of money to charities online. The term is derisive and implies that the impact these actions have on their intended cause is likewise "nano"—imperceptibly small.

netizen: A combination of "network" and "citizen," this term describes anyone who uses the Internet to engage in and foster relationships with communities. Whether for intellectual stimulation or social banter, netizens communicate with other online users with a variety of tools, including blogs, email, Facebook, Twitter, and a host of other social networks.

netroots: A combination of "Internet" and "grassroots," the term refers to political activists who organize through online social media. It is particularly associated with progressives in the United States. The annual Netroots Nation convention, which seeks to be the center of this movement, is an outgrowth of a yearly meeting of people associated with the influential progressive blog "DailyKos."

online organizing: The use of the Internet to increase the effectiveness of the community organizing model, a system developed by trade unions that defines how grassroots organizations should advance the political interests of their members. Like community organizing, online organizing includes recruitment though personal networks, volunteer labor, and empowerment of community leaders. While strategies remain largely the same as in the pre-Internet era, these activities are now supported by digital tools like email, social networks, sophisticated supporter databases, and online events tools.

open source: A means of producing software in which the source code is accessible to anyone who wishes to examine or improve it. Because open source code is freely accessible, the resulting software is also often available for free to the end user. This practice of software production differs from a closed or proprietary means of production—wherein code is a closely guarded secret and considered to be the intellectual property of the firm

developing the software. Software developed in a closed system is most often sold by the developing company at a profit.

online activism: The practice of using the Internet to increase the effectiveness of a social or political change campaign.

phishing: An illegal attempt to acquire sensitive, personal information by falsely assuming the identity of a person or organization trusted by the recipient of an online communication. A common example of phishing is to send mass emails requesting banking information or usernames and passwords for email accounts.

SIM card: A device found in mobile phones, usually a small piece of plastic, that contains the subscriber identity module (SIM) that uniquely identifies a user to the mobile phone network on which his or her calls are routed. The card holds personal identity information such as a user's phone number, email accounts, and text messages and can be switched between different phones, thus allowing a user to make calls from multiple handsets while retaining the same phone number and contact information.

smart mob: A type of rational yet loosely connected social organization, made possible by the ubiquity of networked communication devices. Such devices and their associated information-sharing practices allow for self-structuring among members. The term was coined in 2002 by Howard Rheingold. The flashmob is a type of smart mob.

SMS: Short message service (SMS), also referred to as texting or text messaging, allows for short messages, usually 140 characters in length, to be sent from one mobile phone to another or between an online application, like Twitter, and a mobile phone.

social media: Content designed to be distributed through social interactions between creators. Because this type of media dissemination requires accessible and easy-to-use content-creation tools and cheap and effective means of transmission, social media are almost always created and distributed through digital networks, Popular social media applications include Flickr (photo sharing), YouTube (video sharing), and Facebook (sharing of multiple content types). This type of media can be created on a variety of devices—from mobile phones to digital music players to computers. Social media challenges the traditional broadcast model of media dissemination because content can be created and shared widely at little expense, making the generation and use of the cultural space more participatory than was possible previously.

sousveillance: Either observing and recording an activity as a participant rather than an onlooker, or reverse surveillance—watching the watcher. In the field of digital activism, the latter meaning is more commonly employed because social media provide many opportunities for activists to observe and report on the activities of political authorities—who usually are in the position of monitoring activists.

splog: A combination of "spam" and "blog" referring to a blog that is created specifically to promote other websites—sometimes by improving the search-engine ranking of the associated sites through linking or by displaying advertising.

technological determinism: The controversial belief that technology makes certain inevitable contributions to society's development that are beyond the control of individuals.

thumb drive (or flash drive): Small portable data storage device, usually the size and shape of a thumb. They are generally rewriteable, come with different storage capacities, and hold memory without a power supply. Thumb drives will fit into any USB (universal serial bus) port on a computer.

Twitter bomb: The process of flooding the micro-blogging site Twitter with similar hashtags, keywords, and links using multiple accounts, with the objective of attracting more viewers to a website, product, service, or idea.

Webcam: A combination of the words "Web" and "camera," this is a small digital video camera meant for use with a computer connected to the Internet. The Webcam is most often used for videoconferencing and video chat.

viral: Describes a piece of content that spreads quickly online as users forward and share it with their friends and acquaintances, much as viruses are transmitted from person to person offline. Viral content transmission online is often associated with online social networks. The high volume, fast dissemination, and low cost of viral transmission make it extremely appealing as a means of increasing brand visibility, product sales, personal promotion, or cause awareness. A humorous or thought-provoking video, blog post, discussion board article, or tweet are among the types of content most likely to go viral, though the exact mechanics of viral spread are hard to manufacture.

About the Authors

Katharine Brodock is a new media marketing specialist and founder of the marketing strategy firm Other Side Group. She holds an MBA from the Goizueta Business School of Emory University, an MA in international relations from The Fletcher School of Tufts University, and two BAs—one in history and the other in political science from the University of Rochester. She now works with new media to develop marketing strategies that best fit into a digital world. She is in the Strategy Group for the Meta-Activism Project, is the managing director of the Girls in Tech Boston Chapter, works with the Boston World Partnership, and is involved in a variety of research projects on the topic of using digital tools for political, societal, or cultural influence.

Simon Columbus is a freelance writer and activist based in Berlin. He has campaigned for privacy and data security within the Arbeitskreis Vorratsdatenspeicherung and cofounded the Privacy Workshop Project. His writings on Internet politics, digital activism, and free culture are frequently published in online media such as netzpolitik.org and gulli:news.

Brannon Cullum is a recent graduate of Georgetown University's Master's program in communication, culture, and technology. Her master's thesis is entitled "The Transformative Power of Mobile Technologies: Efforts to Harness the Poverty-Reducing Potential of ICTs by Engaging Local Stakeholders in Least Developed Countries." She holds a bachelor's degree in American studies from Stanford University. Prior to entering graduate school, Brannon taught global studies and English in Texas.

Sem Devillart is cofounder and managing partner of Popular Operations, a firm dedicated to the practice and application of futurism in the commercial and social development sectors.

Sem has pursued her passion for trend analysis and future fore-casting around the world at organizations like Studio Edelkoort, Faith Popcorn's BrainReserve, and the BBC. A few years ago, she moved from London to New York to concentrate on developing methods to track, quantify, and map cultural change as a basis for business strategy. Sem studied art history, sociology, comparative religion, and design in Tübingen (Germany) and Milan. She is a faculty member of the branding program at the School of Visual Arts in New York City.

Tom Glaisyer is a Knight Media policy fellow at the New America Foundation, is currently enrolled in the Graduate School of Jour-nalism at Columbia University, and is completing a doctorate; his thesis considers communications within digital society and the institutions, policies, and practices that surround it. He holds a bachelor's degree in engineering and economics from the Uni-versity of Birmingham (UK) and a master's in international affairs from The School of Public and International Affairs at Columbia University. He can be contacted at teg2102@columbia.edu.

Tim Hwang is the founder and current director of the Web Ecol-ogy Project, a research community dedicated to building an ap-plied science around measuring and influencing the system-wide flows of culture and patterns of community formation online. He currently works as a social metrics analyst with The Barbarian Group; formerly, he was a researcher with the Berkman Center for Internet and Society at Harvard University. Articles about him and his work have appeared in the *Washington Post, Wired Magazine*, the *New York Times*, and the *Boston Globe*, among others. He is also the creator of ROFLCon, a series of conferences celebrating and examining Internet culture and celebrity. Currently, he serves as the chair for higher awesome studies at the Awesome Foundation for the Arts and Sciences, a philanthropic organization founded to provide grants to projects that forward the interest of awesome-ness in the universe. He currently Twitters @timhwang, and blogs regularly at BrosephStalin.com.

Mary Joyce is a pioneer in the field of digital activism and travels the world training, speaking, and consulting on the topic. She is the founder of the Meta-Activism Project, which seeks to develop a new body of activism knowledge that recognizes the radically different communications infrastructure of the digitally networked world. She is also the cofounder of DigiActive, an organization that helps grassroots activists around the world use digital technology more effectively. In 2008, Mary was chosen to act as new media operations manager for the campaign of Pres. Barack Obama. She can be reached at MaryCJoyce@gmail.com.

Andreas Jungherr is pursuing his doctorate in political science at the University of Bamberg (Germany), where he teaches courses in political communication and the sociology of elections. He holds an artium magister in political science from the University of Mainz (Germany). He is a member of the German Christian Democratic Union and has held leadership positions in multiple German online campaigns. These campaigns include political races at the state and local levels in Germany as well as state and nationwide online campaigns. He has presented peer-reviewed papers on the role of digital tools for political activists and political parties at various international conferences. He is also the author of "The DigiActive Guide to Twitter for Activism", a handbook available for download at DigiActive.org.

Dave Karpf is a postdoctoral research associate at Brown University's Taubman Center for Public Policy, having completed his doctorate in political science at the University of Pennsylvania in 2009. He is the author of multiple academic articles on the emergence of netroots political associations in the United States. Prior to entering academia, Dave served as national director of the Sierra Student Coalition, the student-run arm of the Sierra Club. Beginning in 2004, he served on the Sierra Club's national board of directors. His research can be found online at www.davidkarpf.com.

Anastasia Kavada is a research fellow at the Communication and Media Research Institute of the University of Westminster (UK). She earned an MA in communication and a PhD in media and communication from Westminster. Her doctoral thesis examined the global justice movement and its use of the Internet, focusing on the European Social Forum, one of the most important events organized by the movement in Europe. Anastasia's research interests encompass the role of the Internet in the establishment of international campaigns and activist networks, in practices of decentralized organizing and participatory democracy, as well as in the development of solidarity and a sense of common identity among participants in collective action. Anastasia's articles have appeared or are forthcoming in a variety of edited books and peer-reviewed journals, including *Information, Communication and Society* and *Media, Culture and Society.*

Steven Murdoch is a researcher at the University of Cambridge and fellow of Christ's College. He holds a doctorate in computing, for which he studied anonymous communication network security, a method of guarding a user's privacy online. Following his doctoral studies, Steven worked with the OpenNet Initiative, a joint project of Harvard, Cambridge and Oxford, and the University of Toronto, where he surveyed the state of worldwide Internet censorship. He now works on the Tor Project, one of the leading anonymous communication networks, conducting research on how to improve the performance, usability, and security of the system. He also trains human rights defenders on computer and network security, as well as on how to protect their online privacy and circumvent censorship. Steven's other areas of interest include smart card and banking security; he is chief security architect of Cronto, an online authentication technology provider. He maintains a website at http://www.cl.cam.ac.uk/users/ sjm217/; he blogs at http://www. lightbluetouchpaper.org/

Rasmus Kleis Nielsen is a doctoral student in communications at the Graduate School of Journalism at Columbia University. His research focuses on the intersections between new technologies and old organizations, in particular in political campaigns and the news media. He holds bachelor's and master's degrees in political science from the University of Copenhagen and a master's degree in political theory from the University of Essex (UK); he has previously worked for the Danish government and as the managing editor of the social science quarterly *Tidsskriftet Politik*. He can be reached at rasmuskleisnielsen@gmail.com

Trebor Scholz teaches in the department of culture and media studies at Eugene Lang College at The New School for Liberal Arts in New York City. He graduated from the Art Academy in Dresden (Germany), University College London (UK), The Whitney Museum Independent Study Program, the Hochschule für Kunst und Gestaltung in Zürich (Switzerland), and The University of Plymouth (UK). Trebor's research interests focus on social media, especially in education, art, and media activism outside the United States and Europe. In 2004, he founded the Institute for Distributed Creativity. Its mailing list, which he moderates, is a leading discussion forum in network culture. Trebor has also convened several major conferences including Kosova: Carnival in the Eye of the Storm (2000), Free Cooperation (2004), and The Internet as Playground and Factory (2009).

Dan Schultz was awarded his undergraduate degree in information systems by Carnegie Mellon University in 2009. In 2007, he was selected to be a grantee in the Knight News Challenge to blog on the PBS IdeaLab about Connecting People, Content, and Community, where he explored the potential of digital technology as a community catalyst. As a member of DigiActive, Dan authored "A DigiActive Introduction to Facebook Activism" and took the role of lead editor for "A DigiActive Guide to Twitter." Both handbooks are available on the DigiActive site. He is currently developing a community website, The Globally Personalized Forum.

Brian Waniewski is cofounder and managing partner of Popular Operations, a firm dedicated to the practice and application of futurism in the commercial and social development sectors. Throughout his career, Brian has pursued his passion for beauty, harmony, and communication in academic, corporate, and nonprofit settings around the world. Before starting Popular Operations, he worked at Faith Popcorn's BrainReserve in New York, where he led the development and launch of a new product line to deliver cultural intelligence to *Fortune* 100 clients, including PepsiCo, Unilever, and Johnson & Johnson. He also directed The Monday Campaigns, a nonprofit public health project in association with the Johns Hopkins University. Brian studied history and English literature in the United States and Germany.

Talia Whyte is editor of DigiActive. She is also a freelance journalist who has been writing about issues related to social justice, media, and technology for more than ten years. Some of her writing can be found in the *Boston Globe, Houston Chronicle, Real Clear Politics, The Progressive, The Grio*, and many others. She is the founder and director of Global Wire Associates, an international initiative to promote innovative communication for advancing social justice.